Teach Yourself VISUALLY™

iMac™

Visual™

From
maranGraphics™

&

 IDG Books Worldwide, Inc.
IDG An International Data Group Company
BOOKS Foster City, CA • Indianapolis • Chicago • New York

D1288432

Teach Yourself VISUALLY™ iMac™

Published by
IDG Books Worldwide, Inc.
An International Data Group Company
919 E. Hillsdale Blvd., Suite 400
Foster City, CA 94404
www.idgbooks.com (IDG Books Worldwide Web Site)

Library of Congress Control Number: 00-107554

ISBN: 0-7645-3453-X

Printed in the United States of America

10 9 8 7 6 5 4 3 2 1

1K/QW/QZ/QQ/IN

Distributed in the United States by IDG Books Worldwide, Inc.

Distributed by CDG Books Canada Inc. for Canada; by Transworld Publishers Limited in the United Kingdom; by IDG Norge Books for Norway; by IDG Sweden Books for Sweden; by IDG Books Australia Publishing Corporation Pty. Ltd. for Australia and New Zealand; by TransQuest Publishers Pte Ltd. for Singapore, Malaysia, Thailand, Indonesia, and Hong Kong; by Gotop Information Inc. for Taiwan; by ICG Muse, Inc. for Japan; by Intersoft for South Africa; by Eyrolles for France; by International Thomson Publishing for Germany, Austria and Switzerland; by Distribuidora Cuspide for Argentina; by LR International for Brazil; by Galileo Libros for Chile; by Ediciones ZETA S.C.R. Ltda. for Peru; by WS Computer Publishing Corporation, Inc., for the Philippines; by Contemporanea de Ediciones for Venezuela; by Express Computer Distributors for the Caribbean and West Indies; by Micronesia Media Distributor, Inc. for Micronesia; by Chips Computadoras S.A. de C.V. for Mexico; by Editorial Norma de Panama S.A. for Panama; by American Bookshops for Finland.

For corporate orders, please call maranGraphics at 800-469-6616.

For general information on IDG Books Worldwide's books in the U.S., please call our Consumer Customer Service department at 800-762-2974. For reseller information, including discounts and premium sales, please call our Reseller Customer Service department at 800-434-3422.

For information on where to purchase IDG Books Worldwide's books outside the U.S., please contact our International Sales department at 317-572-3993 or fax 317-572-4002.

For consumer information on foreign language translations, please contact our Customer Service department at 1-800-434-3422, fax 317-572-4002, or e-mail rights@idgbooks.com.

For information on licensing foreign or domestic rights, please phone +1-650-653-7098.

For sales inquiries and special prices for bulk quantities, please contact our Order Services department at 800-434-3422 or write to the address above.

For information on using IDG Books Worldwide's books in the classroom or for ordering examination copies, please contact our Educational Sales department at 800-434-2086 or fax 317-572-4005.

For press review copies, author interviews, or other publicity information, please contact our Public Relations department at 650-653-7000 or fax 650-653-7500.

For authorization to photocopy items for corporate, personal, or educational use, please contact Copyright Clearance Center, 222 Rosewood Drive, Danvers, MA 01923, or fax 978-750-4470.

Screen shots displayed in this book are based on pre-released software and are subject to change.

Trademark Acknowledgments

Permissions

Apple

maranGraphics

U.S. Corporate Sales	U.S. Trade Sales
Contact maranGraphics at (800) 469-6616 or Fax (905) 890-9434.	Contact IDG Books at (800) 434-3422 or (650) 655-3000.

ABOUT IDG BOOKS WORLDWIDE

Welcome to the world of IDG Books Worldwide.

IDG Books Worldwide, Inc., is a subsidiary of International Data Group, the world's largest publisher of computer-related information and the leading global provider of information services on information technology. IDG was founded more than 30 years ago by Patrick J. McGovern and now employs more than 9,000 people worldwide. IDG publishes more than 290 computer publications in over 75 countries. More than 90 million people read one or more IDG publications each month.

Launched in 1990, IDG Books Worldwide is today the #1 publisher of best-selling computer books in the United States. We are proud to have received eight awards from the Computer Press Association in recognition of editorial excellence and three from Computer Currents' First Annual Readers' Choice Awards. Our best-selling ...*For Dummies*® series has more than 50 million copies in print with translations in 31 languages. IDG Books Worldwide, through a joint venture with IDG's Hi-Tech Beijing, became the first U.S. publisher to publish a computer book in the People's Republic of China. In record time, IDG Books Worldwide has become the first choice for millions of readers around the world who want to learn how to better manage their businesses.

Our mission is simple: Every one of our books is designed to bring extra value and skill-building instructions to the reader. Our books are written by experts who understand and care about our readers. The knowledge base of our editorial staff comes from years of experience in publishing, education, and journalism — experience we use to produce books to carry us into the new millennium. In short, we care about books, so we attract the best people. We devote special attention to details such as audience, interior design, use of icons, and illustrations. And because we use an efficient process of authoring, editing, and desktop publishing our books electronically, we can spend more time ensuring superior content and less time on the technicalities of making books.

You can count on our commitment to deliver high-quality books at competitive prices on topics you want to read about. At IDG Books Worldwide, we continue in the IDG tradition of delivering quality for more than 30 years. You'll find no better book on a subject than one from IDG Books Worldwide.

IDG BOOKS WORLDWIDE

John Kilcullen
Chairman and CEO
IDG Books Worldwide, Inc.

Eighth Annual Computer Press Awards ≥1992

Ninth Annual Computer Press Awards ≥1993

Tenth Annual Computer Press Awards ≥1994

Eleventh Annual Computer Press Awards ≥1995

**maranGraphics is a family-run business
located near Toronto, Canada.**

At **maranGraphics**, we believe in producing great computer books — one book at a time.

maranGraphics has been producing high-technology products for over 25 years, which enables us to offer the computer book community a unique communication process.

Our computer books use an integrated communication process, which is very different from the approach used in other computer books. Each spread is, in essence, a flow chart — the text and screen shots are totally incorporated into the layout of the spread. Introductory text and helpful tips complete the learning experience.

maranGraphics' approach encourages the left and right sides of the brain to work together — resulting in faster orientation and greater memory retention.

Above all, we are very proud of the handcrafted nature of our books. Our carefully chosen writers are experts in their fields, and spend countless hours researching and organizing the content for each topic. Our artists rebuild every screen shot to provide the best clarity possible, making our screen shots the most precise and easiest to read in the

industry. We strive for perfection, and believe that the time spent handcrafting each element results in the best computer books money can buy.

Thank you for purchasing this book. We hope you enjoy it!

Sincerely,

Robert Maran
President
maranGraphics
Rob@maran.com
www.maran.com
www.idgbooks.com/visual

CREDITS

Acquisitions, Editorial, and Media Development

Project Editors:
Ted Cains, Darren Meiss

Acquisitions Editor:
Martine Edwards

Associate Project Coordinator:
Lindsay Sandman

Proof Editor:
Dwight Ramsey

Technical Editor:
Dennis R. Cohen

Editorial Manager:
Rev Mengle

Media Development Managers:
Heather Heath Dismore, Laura Carpenter

Editorial Assistant:
Candace Nicholson

Production

Book Design:
maranGraphics™

Project Coordinator:
Valery Bourke

Layout:
Joe Bucki, Barry Offringa, Kathie Schutte

Editorial Graphics Production:
Ronda David-Burroughs, Craig Dearing,
David Gregory, Mark Harris, Jill Johnson

Proofreaders:
Laura Albert, Sally Burton, Marianne Santy

Indexer:
Maro Riofranco

Special Help:
Clint Lahnen, Brent Savage,
Anthony Stuart

ACKNOWLEDGMENTS

General and Administrative

IDG Books Worldwide, Inc.: John Kilcullen, CEO

IDG Books Technology Publishing Group: Richard Swadley, Senior Vice President and Publisher; Walter R. Bruce III, Vice President and Publisher; Joseph Wikert, Vice President and Publisher; Mary Bednarek, Vice President and Director, Product Development; Andy Cummings, Publishing Director, General User Group; Mary C. Corder, Editorial Director; Barry Pruett, Publishing Director

IDG Books Consumer Publishing Group: Roland Elgey, Senior Vice President and Publisher; Kathleen A. Welton, Vice President and Publisher; Kevin Thornton, Acquisitions Manager; Kristin A. Cocks, Editorial Director

IDG Books Internet Publishing Group: Brenda McLaughlin, Senior Vice President and Publisher; Sofia Marchant, Online Marketing Manager

IDG Books Production for Branded Press: Debbie Stailey, Director of Production; Cindy L. Phipps, Manager of Project Coordination, Production Proofreading, and Indexing; Tony Augsburger, Manager of Prepress, Reprints, and Systems; Shelley Lea, Supervisor of Graphics and Design; Debbie J. Gates, Production Systems Specialist; Robert Springer, Supervisor of Proofreading; Trudy Coler, Page Layout Manager; Kathie Schutte, Senior Page Layout Supervisor; Janet Seib, Page Layout Supervisor; Michael Sullivan, Production Supervisor

Packaging and Book Design: Patty Page, Manager, Promotions Marketing

The publisher would like to give special thanks to Patrick J. McGovern,
without whom this book would not have been possible.

ABOUT THE AUTHOR

Mark L. Chambers has been an author, computer consultant, BBS sysop, programmer, and hardware technician for more than 15 years. His first love affair with a computer peripheral blossomed in 1984, when he bought his lightning-fast 300 BPS modem. Now he spends entirely too much time on the Internet and drinks far too much caffeine. His favorite pastimes include collecting gargoyles, watching St. Louis Cardinal baseball games, playing his three pinball machines and the latest computer games, fixing and upgrading computers, and rendering three-dimensional flights of fancy with TrueSpace. And during all that, he listens to just about every type of music imaginable.

With a degree in journalism and creative writing from Louisiana State University, Mark took the logical career choice and started programming computers. However, after five years as a COBOL programmer for a hospital system, he decided that there must be a better way to earn a living, and he became the documentation manager for a well-known communications software developer. Somewhere in between organizing and writing software manuals, Mark began writing computer books; his first book, *Running a Perfect BBS*, was published in 1994. He now writes several books a year and edits whatever his publishers throw at him. You can reach him by visiting his book site on the Web at www.geocities.com/SiliconValley/Bay/4373/index.html. He welcomes all comments and questions about his books.

Mark's other books include *The Hewlett-Packard Official Printer Handbook, The Hewlett-Packard Official Recordable CD Handbook, Computer Gamer's Bible, Building a PC For Dummies, Recordable CD Bible, Official Netscape Guide to Web Animation,* and the *Windows 98 Troubleshooting and Optimizing Little Black Book.*

AUTHORS ACKNOWLEDGMENTS

Most of the books I've written have required several paragraphs to thank everyone involved. This book, however, has been a very personal project among only a handful of very dedicated and hard-working people.

First, I'd like to thank (once again!) Martine Edwards, my acquisitions editor for this title. It takes many hours of work to launch a book, and Martine weaved her magic yet again in conceiving and planning this material.

My thanks also to Lindsay Sandman, associate project coordinator for the Visual series, for keeping everyone on course throughout the project.

I'd also like to thank IDB Books' Production Department for assembling the book's layout and the Editorial Graphics Production team (Ronda David-Burroughs, Craig Dearing, David Gregory, Mark Harris, and Jill Johnson) and a number of fine freelance artists for creating the graphics for this book.

As with every book I've written, I'd like to thank my wife, Anne, and my children Erin, Chelsea, and Rose, for their continued support and love — and for letting me follow my dream!

And finally, I come to the three guys who worked the hardest: My heartfelt thanks to my project editors Ted Cains and Darren Meiss, and to my editorial manager Rev Mengle. Without their guidance and attention to detail, this title would never have been possible. I know you'll find this book both easy to read and a visual work of art, but it took many months of complex editing and formatting on their part — and probably a bottle or two of pain reliever to boot — to fashion the finished pages. To all three of them, I send my best!

Mark L. Chambers

TABLE OF CONTENTS

Chapter 3

Chapter 4

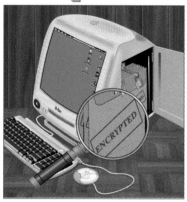

TABLE OF CONTENTS

Chapter 5

Chapter 6

Chapter 7

Chapter 8

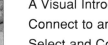

CONNECTING TO THE INTERNET

Chapter 9

BROWSING THE WEB

TABLE OF CONTENTS

Chapter 10

WORKING WITH E-MAIL

Chapter 11

USING SHERLOCK 2

Chapter 12

UPGRADING YOUR IMAC

Chapter 13

OPTIMIZING YOUR IMAC

Chapter 14

TROUBLESHOOTING PROBLEMS

CHAPTER 1

Meet Your iMac

The iMac is the easiest computer to set up, and this chapter shows you all the tricks to do just that.

iMac

UNPACK YOUR iMAC

Although most people do not think about it, there is a right way and a wrong way to unpack your iMac. Following this procedure can save you time and trouble later.

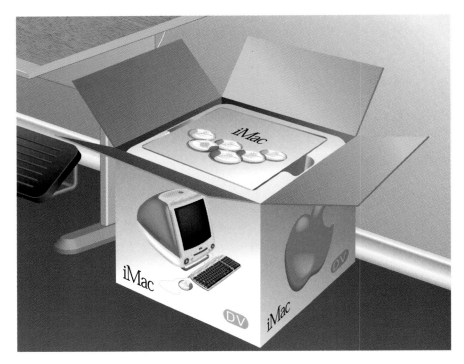

1. Check the outside of the box for obvious damage, such as large punctures or crush marks. Make a note of their location and contact the store if the computer is damaged.

2. Open the iMac's box, remove all the packing materials and accessory boxes, and set them aside.

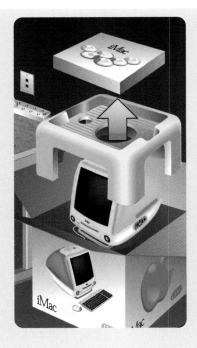

3 Carefully lift the iMac out of the box by the handle and place it on the floor or a table.

4 Remove any protective plastic from your iMac's case, keyboard, and mouse.

5 The top and bottom of your iMac may be covered in a thin layer of plastic. Peel this off.

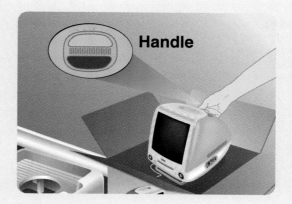

Handle

6 Remove all the accessories and check the packing materials for any small parts they may contain.

7 Replace the packing in the iMac box.

8 Store the iMac box in a safe place — if your iMac needs to be replaced or serviced, you will need it to ship or carry your computer.

CHOOSE A HOME FOR YOUR iMAC

Your iMac needs a
home with the proper
connections and the proper
ventilation. The right spot
should be ergonomically
correct, too.

If you plan to use the modem,
you need a phone jack
nearby.

Note: If you plan to hook the
iMac up to a network, you
need an Ethernet CAT5 port
nearby.

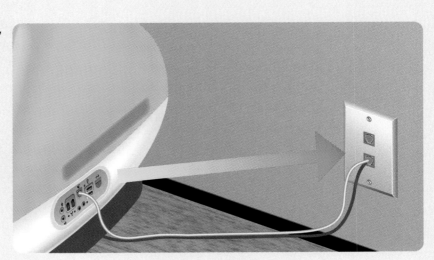

Use a surge protector to provide extra AC outlets for a printer, external drive, or scanner.

Your iMac's screen should be at eye level when you're sitting. If necessary, place the computer on a raised surface to bring it to eye level.

You can reduce the risk of carpal tunnel syndrome if your keyboard is level with your elbows.

Keyboard and mouse wrist rests also help prevent strain on your wrists.

Your iMac gives off heat as you use it, so it needs lots of space for proper ventilation. Make sure that your iMac has at least six inches of space all around the case.

iMAC HARDWARE

Unlike most computers, the iMac integrates its main parts into a single case with an integrated handle. As a result, it's easy to carry and takes up very little space.

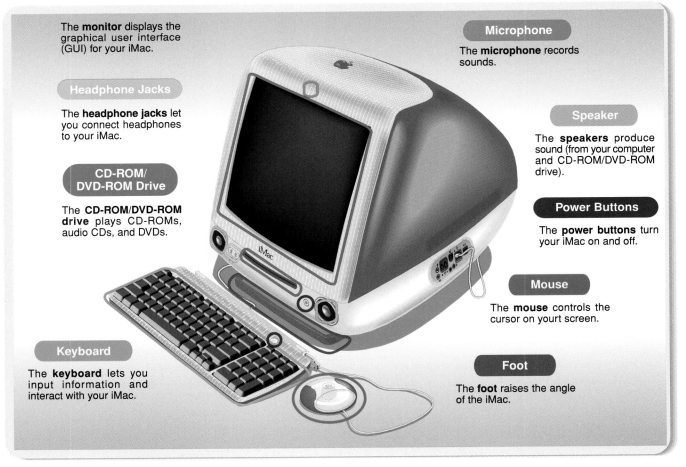

The **monitor** displays the graphical user interface (GUI) for your iMac.

Headphone Jacks

The **headphone jacks** let you connect headphones to your iMac.

CD-ROM/ DVD-ROM Drive

The **CD-ROM/DVD-ROM drive** plays CD-ROMs, audio CDs, and DVDs.

Keyboard

The **keyboard** lets you input information and interact with your iMac.

Microphone

The **microphone** records sounds.

Speaker

The **speakers** produce sound (from your computer and CD-ROM/DVD-ROM drive).

Power Buttons

The **power buttons** turn your iMac on and off.

Mouse

The **mouse** controls the cursor on yourt screen.

Foot

The **foot** raises the angle of the iMac.

What is USB?

USB stands for *Universal Serial Bus*, which is the new, universal standard for connecting peripheral devices, such as printers and scanners, to computers. Most USB devices can be used on both Windows PCs and Macintosh computers with USB ports.

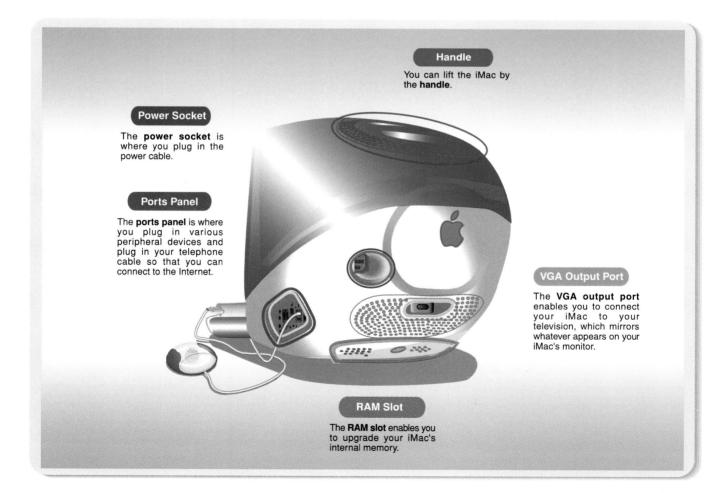

Handle

You can lift the iMac by the **handle**.

Power Socket

The **power socket** is where you plug in the power cable.

Ports Panel

The **ports panel** is where you plug in various peripheral devices and plug in your telephone cable so that you can connect to the Internet.

VGA Output Port

The **VGA output port** enables you to connect your iMac to your television, which mirrors whatever appears on your iMac's monitor.

RAM Slot

The **RAM slot** enables you to upgrade your iMac's internal memory.

iMAC PORTS AND CONNECTORS

Your iMac uses a number of different ports and cables to connect to the outside world.

The power cable fits into a connector at the rear of the iMac. You can connect this cable only one way.

GROUNDED OUTLET

Your iMac requires a three-prong grounded outlet.

MODEM PORT

Your modem uses a standard telephone cable to connect to the wall jack.

USB PORTS

You need to reserve one USB port for your keyboard and mouse.

Other USB peripherals include joysticks, gamepads, scanners, printers, and video cameras. If you run out of USB ports, you can buy a USB *hub*, which provides additional USB ports; you have to have an available USB port to plug the hub into.

HEADPHONES JACK

You can plug in two sets of headphones here.

The iMac automatically turns off the built-in speakers when you connect a set of headphones.

SOUND-OUT JACK

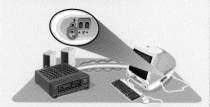

Plug in a set of external speakers to your iMac here or run the sound into your stereo.

The iMac automatically turns off the built-in speakers when you connect a set of external speakers.

SOUND-IN JACK

Plug in an external microphone or a line from your stereo.

ETHERNET PORT

You can connect your iMac to an Ethernet network. You can also connect your iMac to another Macintosh that has an Ethernet port.

The iMac's built-in Ethernet hardware supports both 10 and 100Mbps transfer rates, so your computer is compatible with just about any Ethernet network.

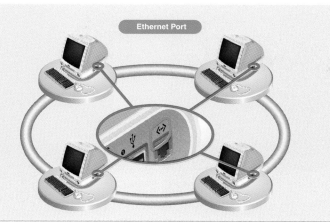

Ethernet Port

CONNECT THE KEYBOARD, MOUSE, AND MODEM

Here's how to put all the pieces together.

CONNECT THE MOUSE

Plug the cable from the mouse into one of the USB ports in the iMac keyboard.

Note: The USB connector only fits one way.

CONNECT THE KEYBOARD

Plug the keyboard into one of the USB ports on the access panel.

CONNECT THE MODEM

Plug one end of the telephone cable into the modem port on the access panel.

Plug the other end of the telephone cable into a wall jack.

Your iMac has an internal modem, which is designed only for a standard telephone line. You can switch to an ISDN or cable modem if you want, but you will need to buy extra equipment for these connections.

ADJUSTING ANGLE

You can adjust both the iMac and the keyboard to two different viewing angles.

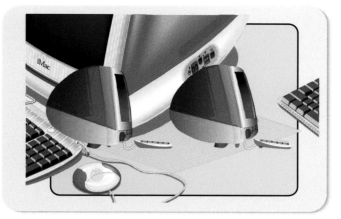

ADJUST THE KEYBOARD ANGLE

Swing the keyboard **foot** out for an angled typing surface.

ADJUST THE SCREEN ANGLE

Carefully lift up the front of the iMac.

Swing the iMac foot to change the monitor angle.

PRINTER STAND

If you've propped up the iMac and it's still not at the correct angle, you can place your iMac on a stand to raise it several inches. Although most printer stands will work, many stores sell pedestals that are designed specifically for iMac.

iMAC CONTROLS

Your iMac has all sorts of buttons to press. Here's what they do.

THE MOUSE BUTTON

The mouse button is the rounded tip of the mouse. Hold the mouse with the button pointing forward. The "top" of the mouse is the area around the mouse button.

If you don't like iMac's mouse, you can purchase a different one. If you'd rather use another style of mouse or a trackball, buy one with a USB connector that specifically supports the iMac.

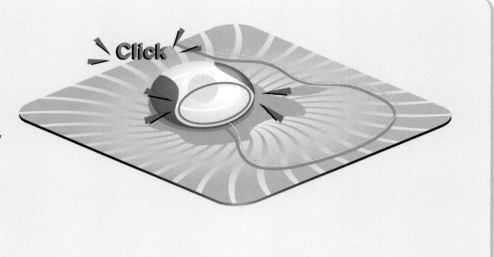

Click

IMAC'S ON/OFF SWITCHES

The iMac has two On/Off switches, and you can use either one to turn your iMac on, turn it off, restart it, or wake it up from sleep mode.

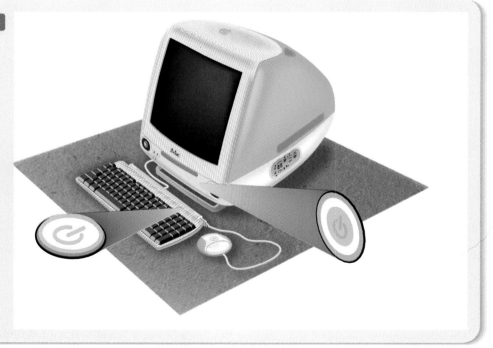

IMAC'S POWER MODES

If the On/Off switch below the
monitor is green, the iMac is
on. If it's red (or pulsing
yellow), the iMac is in sleep
mode. If it's not glowing at all,
your iMac is off.

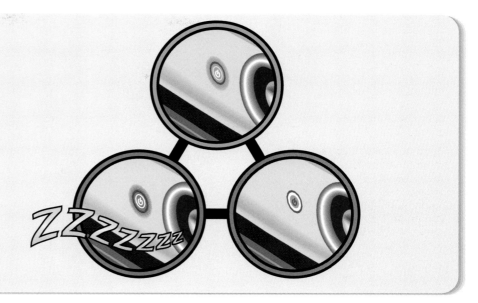

TRAY-LOADING CD-ROM DRIVE

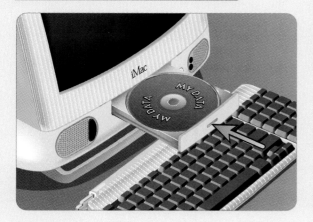

If you have a tray-loading CD-ROM drive, the
button under the monitor pops out the tray so
that you can load or remove a disc.

SLOT-LOADING CD-ROM/DVD-ROM DRIVE.

If you have a slot-loading CD-ROM/DVD-ROM drive,
you simply put the disc into the slot and push gently.

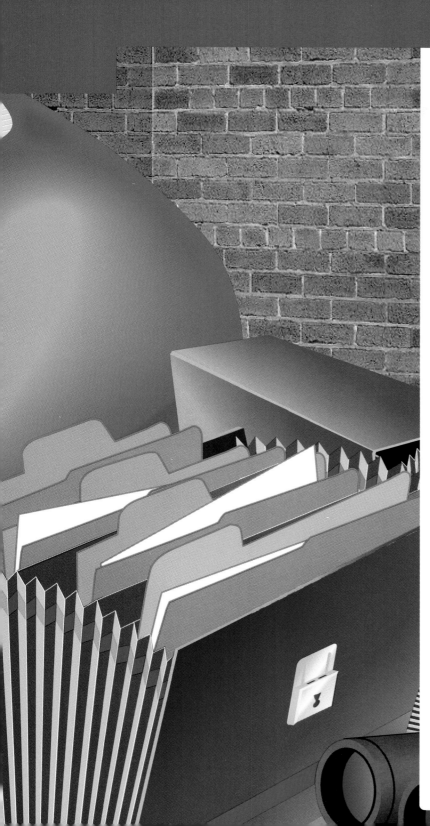

iMac and Mac OS Basics

Wondering what all those funny little things are on your iMac's screen? Wonder no more. This chapter explains all the ins and outs of the Mac OS desktop.

START YOUR iMAC

You can use two buttons to start your iMac.

To start your iMac from the front panel, press the circular power button.

To wake your iMac from sleep mode, click the mouse button or press a key on the keyboard.

Why restart the iMac using the power buttons?

If a program error locks up your iMac, you won't be able to use the Special⇨Restart command. Pressing and holding the power button usually shuts down your iMac even if your mouse doesn't work.

To restart your iMac using either of the power buttons, press and hold the button until the computer turns off, and then press the power button again.

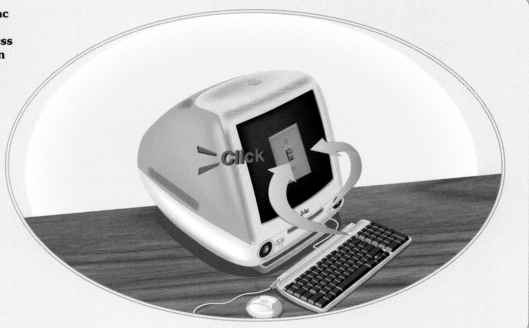

UNDERSTAND ICONS

Icons are symbols on your desktop that represent the files, hardware, and software available on your iMac. Icons enable you to run programs and manage your data without typing cryptic commands.

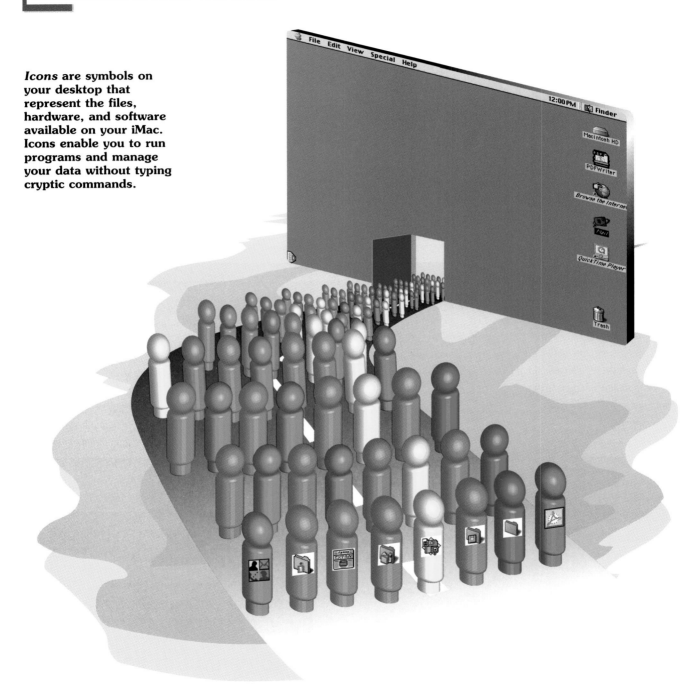

THE MAC OS DESKTOP

**Here's a quick anatomy lesson
on the Mac OS desktop.**

Menu bar

The **menu bar** enables you to access commands for specific applications.

Program

Program icons let you run applications, games, or utility programs.

Hardware

Hardware icons represent your system's hard drive and CD-ROM drive, and they hold other icons that represent the contents of these drives.

File

Your data – such as a word processing document or an address list – is represented by a **file** icon.

Desktop

The desktop is the interface you see after you turn on your iMac; it may have a picture or pattern, and it holds a number of icons.

Folder

Folders store most types of icons – for instance, your financial management program and its data files are likely to be stored in the same folder. Folders make it easier to organize your icons.

Alias

An **alias** is a shortcut to a document or application.

Trash

The **Trash icon** stores files that you want to delete.

WORK WITH ICONS

You can open
documents, move them,
and delete them by
manipulating the icons
that represent them.

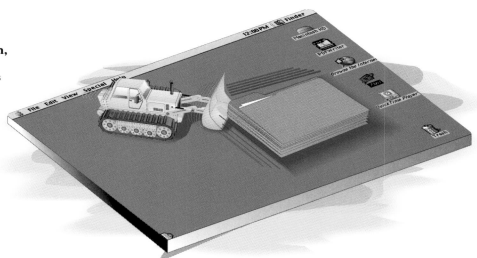

WORK WITH ICONS

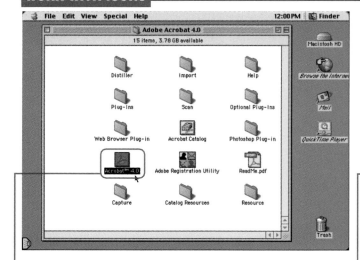

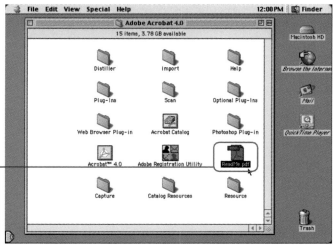

SELECT ICONS

1 To select an icon on your
desktop or within a window,
click it once with your mouse.

■ The icon is highlighted,
indicating that it has been
selected.

OPEN ICONS

1 To open an icon,
double-click it to launch the
application that created it.

How can I rename an icon?
Click once on the icon name to select it. Enter the new name and press the Return key.

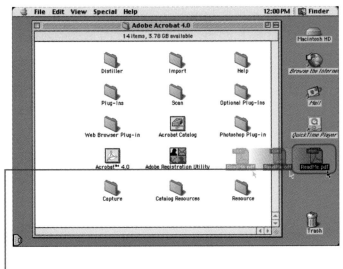

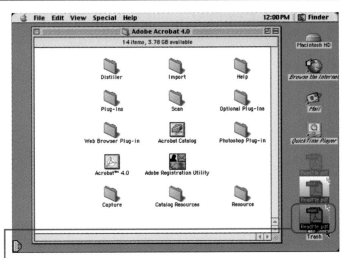

MOVE ICONS

1 To move an icon from one place to another, drag it to the desired spot on your desktop.

■ You can also move the icon into a folder.

DELETE ICONS

1 To delete an icon, drag it to the Trash icon on your desktop.

SELECT MULTIPLE ITEMS WITH YOUR MOUSE

Often, you may want to perform the same operation on more than one file. The iMac enables you to select multiple icons with your mouse.

SELECT MULTIPLE ITEMS WITH YOUR MOUSE

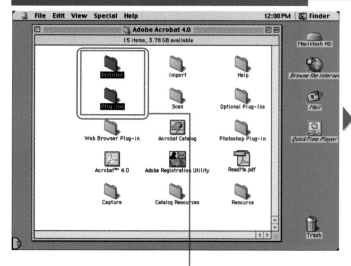

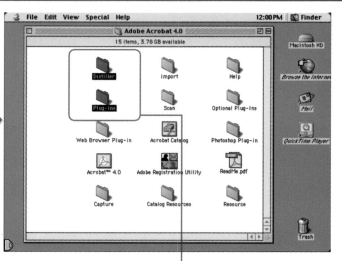

1 If the icons are adjacent to one another, click and drag.

■ A selection box appears around the desired icons.

2 Release the mouse button.

■ The selected icons are highlighted.

How do I move multiple items I've selected?

After you highlight the items, place your cursor over one of the items and click and drag the items.

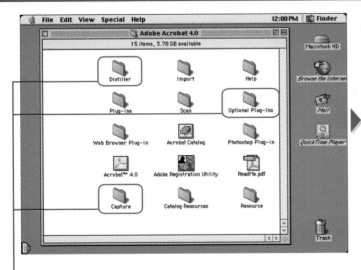

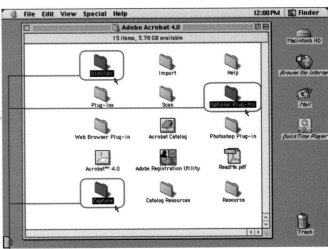

1 If the icons are not adjacent to one another, hold down the Shift key.

2 Click each icon you want to select to highlight it.

SELECT MENU ITEMS

You can control your iMac by using the menu system. Virtually all Macintosh applications use menus.

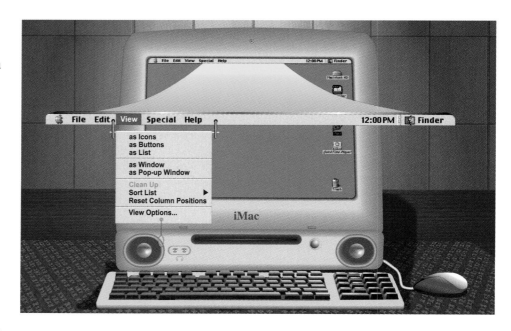

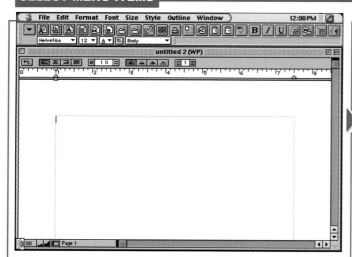

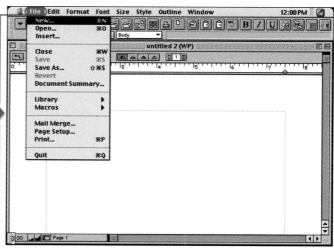

■ The **menu bar** appears along the top of the screen and shows the names of each menu. When you click a menu, the menu expands and you can select a related **menu item**.

■ The **File menu** includes menu items for opening and saving documents, printing, closing documents, and quitting the program.

Does every Macintosh application use the same menu commands?

Not always. Most Macintosh applications use similar menu commands for universal actions, such as quitting, printing, and so on. However, applications also have menu commands that are unique to those programs.

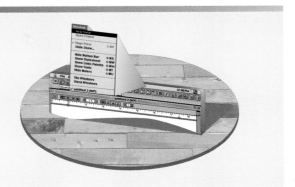

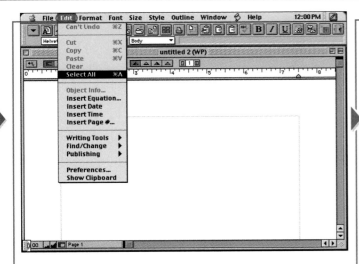

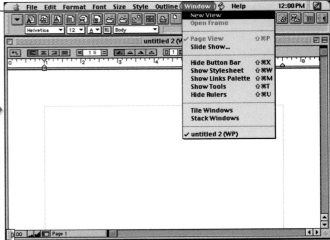

■ The **Edit menu** offers menu items for cutting, pasting, and deleting text; inserting graphics or text; and finding a certain word or phrase.

■ The **Window menu** enables you to switch between multiple documents, hide or display parts of the program's interface (like the button and toolbar), and change the size of the document by zooming in and out.

USING THE BUTTON BAR

Many programs display a strip of buttons that perform the same tasks as the menu items; this strip is called a *button bar*.

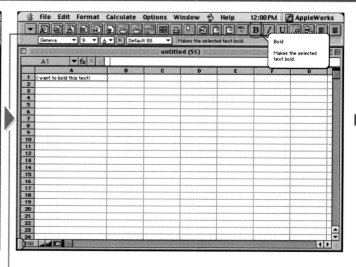

■ This is the AppleWorks button bar.

Note: Depending on the program, the button bar may appear under the menu bar, along the sides of the screen, or even on a "floating" palette.

■ To make the selected text bold, click this button.

How can I determine what a specific button does?

Icons on button bars vary among different programs. Some applications display the name of a button if you let your mouse cursor hover over it.

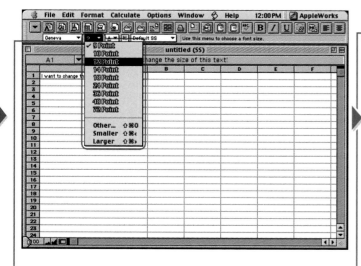

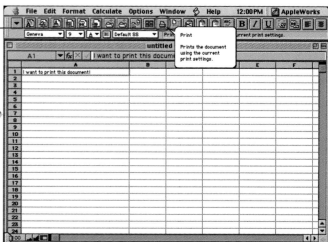

■ To change the size of the text, click the pull-down menu and choose another text size.

■ To print the document, click this button.

USING KEYBOARD SHORTCUTS

Along with button bars, most iMac programs offer convenient keyboard shortcuts for more common commands. Usually, these shortcuts involve holding down one key while pressing another.

Many shortcut sequences use the **Shift key** (which is also used to create capital letters).

The **Control key** does double-duty; besides displaying contextual menus, it's often used in key sequences.

How do I use a shortcut?

To use a keyboard shortcut — for example, ⌘+Q, which quits most Macintosh programs — press and hold the ⌘ key while you press the Q key.

The **Command (⌘) key** is also known as the **Apple key**.

The **Option key** often works in conjunction with the ⌘ key to provide additional functionality.

VIEW FILES

Although programs and files are normally displayed as icons in the Mac OS, that's not the only viewing method. In fact, you can choose from two other viewing formats.

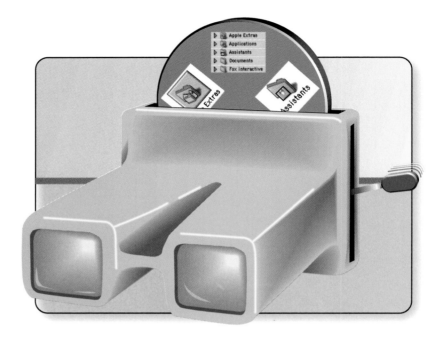

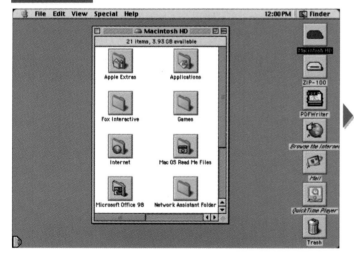

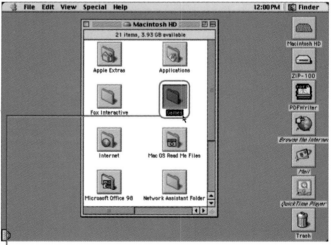

AS BUTTONS

■ When you view the contents of your desktop, folders, and windows as **buttons**, they appear as raised square buttons with icons.

■ A single click opens a folder or launches a program.

How do I change my viewing mode?

You can change your viewing mode by clicking **View** in the menu bar and choosing one of three menu items: **as Icons**, **as Buttons**, and **as List**. Keep in mind that the viewing selection is for only that particular window. If you open a folder in List view, the new folder window appears in the default Icon view.

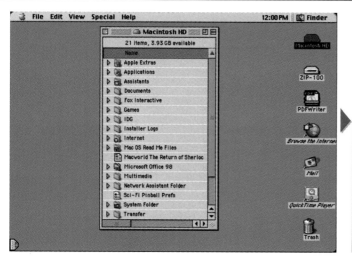

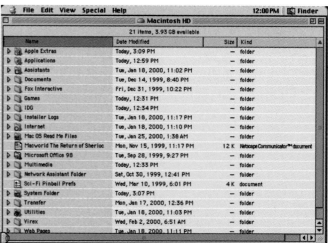

AS LIST

■ In **list** mode, each file appears in a grid with the icon first, followed by the name.

■ The grid also displays the modification date, size, and file type (such as a folder, application, or document).

OPEN FOLDERS

How you open a folder
depends on the viewing
format you use.

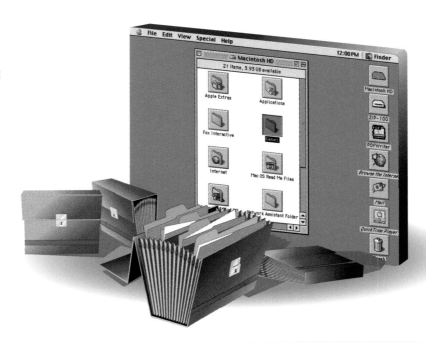

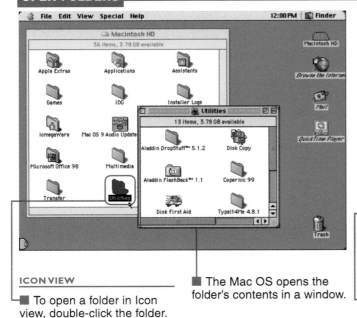

ICON VIEW

■ To open a folder in Icon
view, double-click the folder.

■ The Mac OS opens the
folder's contents in a window.

BUTTON VIEW

■ To open a folder in Button
view, click once on the
button.

■ The Mac OS opens the
folder in a new window.

How can I delete a folder and its contents?

Click and drag the folder icon to the Trash icon and release the mouse button. You can also select the icon and click **File** and choose **Move to Trash.**

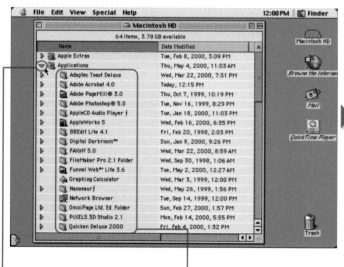

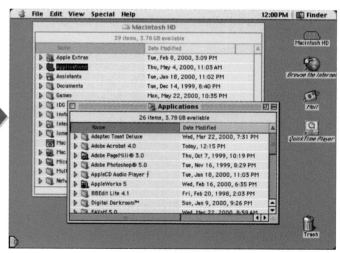

LIST VIEW

■ To view the contents of a folder in List view, click the right-pointing triangle by the folder name.

■ The folder contents appear beneath the folder name.

Note: You can also double-click the folder in List view to see the contents in a new window.

COPY AND MOVE FILES

Copying and moving files on your desktop involves clicking and dragging.

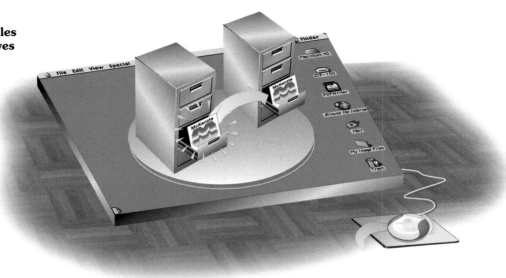

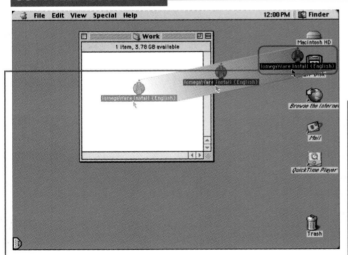

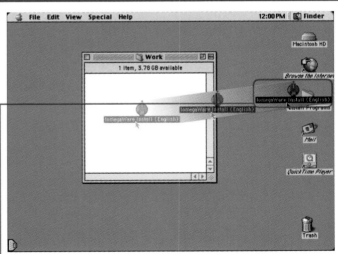

COPY A FILE TO ANOTHER DRIVE

■ To make a copy of a file on another drive (such as a Zip drive), drag its icon onto the drive's icon.

COPY A FILE TO THE SAME DRIVE

■ To make a copy of a file on the same drive in another folder, hold down the Option key while you drag the file icon to the destination folder.

Why does the filename get changed when I duplicate a file?

Because two files in the same location can't share the same name, Mac OS 9 adds the word *copy* to the end of the filename.

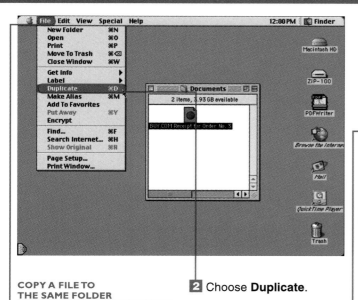

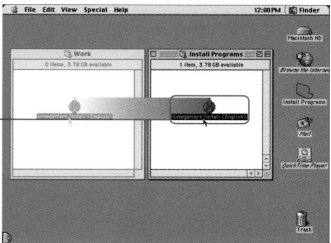

**COPY A FILE TO
THE SAME FOLDER**

■1 To create a copy of a file in the same folder, highlight the file and click **File**.

■2 Choose **Duplicate**.

MOVE A FILE

■ To move a file or folder from one location to another folder, drag its icon onto the destination folder's icon or open window.

MOVE, RESIZE, AND SCROLL WINDOWS

The Mac OS opens *windows* to display many types of information, such as the contents of a folder or the contents of a document. However, you may often want to *move* or *resize* a window, and if you can't see everything in a window, you must *scroll* to see the rest of the contents.

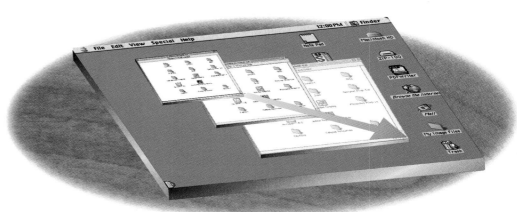

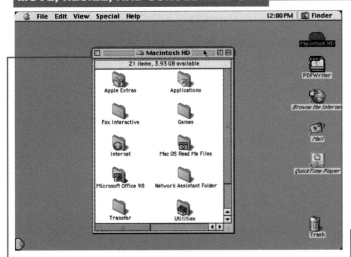

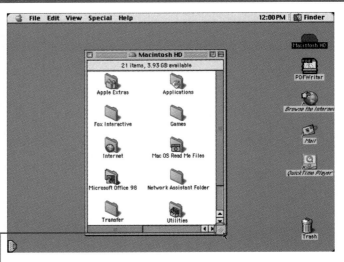

MOVE A WINDOW

◼ Click and drag the **title bar** to move an entire window and all its contents.

RESIZE A WINDOW

◼ Click and drag the **size box** to alter the shape and size of a window.

I need to see a window that's partially hidden by another window. How can I make it active?

To make a window active and bring it to the front, click anywhere within the window frame.

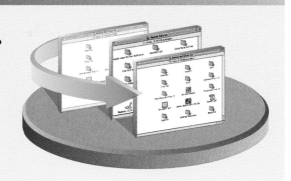

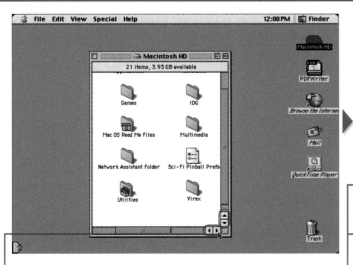

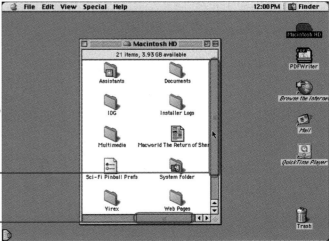

SCROLL THROUGH A WINDOW

■ Click the **scroll arrows** to move the view up and down or left and right within a window.

■ You can also drag the **scroll slider** to scroll.

CLOSE, COLLAPSE, AND HIDE WINDOWS

After you no longer
need the contents of a
window, you can close,
collapse, or hide it.

CLOSE, COLLAPSE, AND HIDE WINDOWS

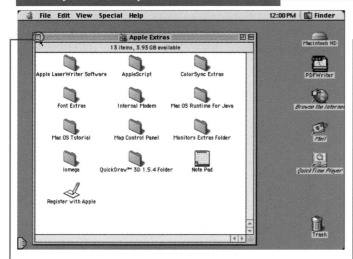

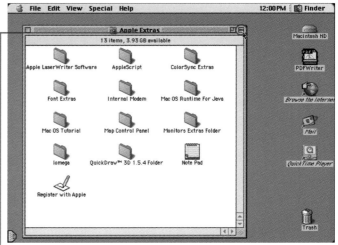

CLOSE A WINDOW

■ To close a window, click
the Close box in the upper-
left corner of the title bar.

COLLAPSE A WINDOW

■ Click the Collapse box to
reduce the window to the
title bar.

If I collapse a program window, does the program continue to run?

Yes. The Mac OS leaves the program running in the background.

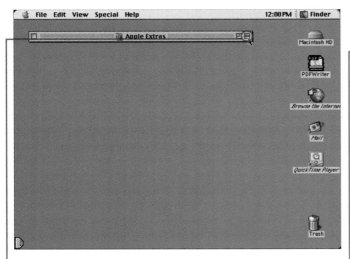

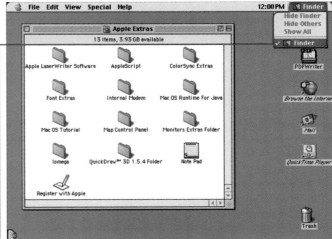

RESTORE A WINDOW

■ Click the Collapse box again to restore a collapsed window to its original size.

HIDE A WINDOW

■ To hide and show windows, click the Application menu at the right end of the menu bar and choose the appropriate option.

USING THE APPLE MENU

The Apple menu is a convenient method of launching your favorite applications and configuring your system settings.

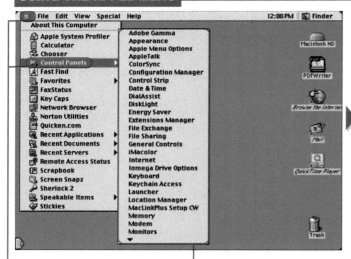

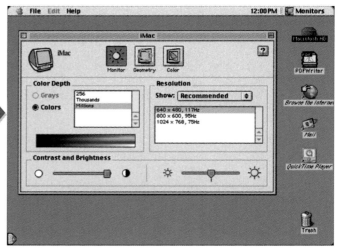

1 Click the Apple menu.

2 Choose **Control Panels** to configure your iMac.

3 Choose a Control Panel to set specific options.

■ With the **Monitor Control Panel**, you can change your monitor resolution, contrast, brightness, and the number of colors.

Can I easily run a program that I used recently or load a document that I closed a few minutes ago?

Yes! The Apple menu includes two submenus: **Recent Applications** and **Recent Documents**. These submenus list the last ten applications and documents that you've accessed.

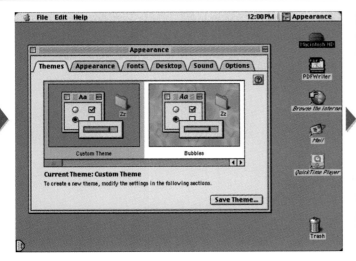

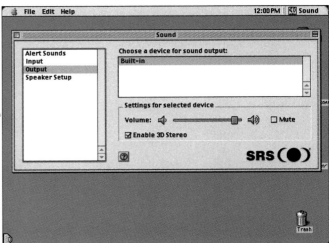

■ With the **Appearance Control Panel**, you can customize the colors, screen fonts, and background of your desktop.

■ With the **Sound Control Panel**, you can choose the alert sound and configure your iMac's microphone and speakers.

Note: To close a Control Panel and save any changes you make, click the Close box in the upper-left corner of the window.

ADD AND REMOVE APPLE MENU ITEMS

For easier access, you can add programs, documents, and folders to your Apple menu.

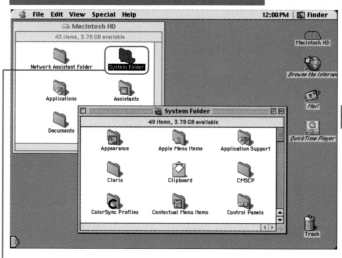

1 Open the System Folder on your hard drive.

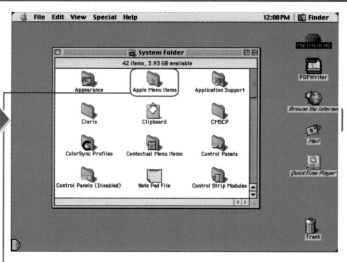

2 Open the Apple Menu Items folder.

**My Apple menu doesn't contain
all the items it usually does.
What's wrong?**

If you boot your iMac from a
CD-ROM, your default Apple menu
items won't load.

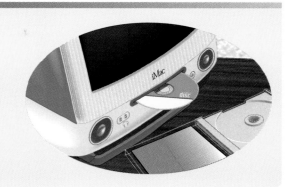

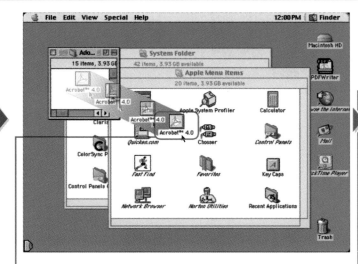

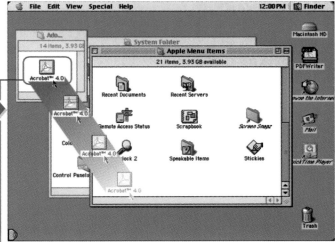

3 Drag the desired icon into
the Apple Menu Items folder.

*Note: You may want to place an
alias of the item in the folder, so
that the original item stays in its
original place.*

4 To remove an Apple
menu item, drag the icon out
of the Apple Menu Items
folder and place it in another
folder or on your desktop.

USING THE CONTROL STRIP

You can use the Control Strip to access many Control Panel settings. To extend the Control Strip, click the tab on the end; to retract it, click the tab again.

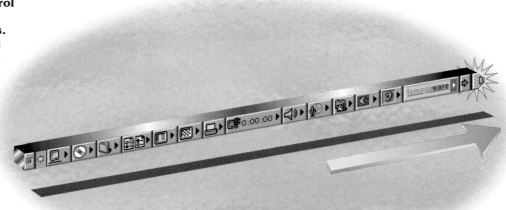

USING THE CONTROL STRIP

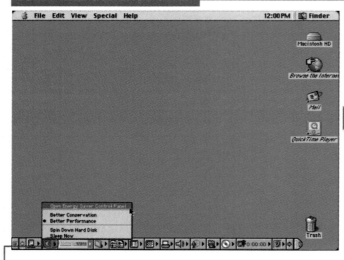

■ To open a Control Strip item, click the button and select the desired function from the pop-up menu.

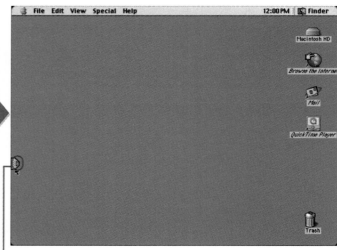

■ To move the Control Strip, hold down the Option key while dragging the tab.

How do I remove an item from the Control Strip?

Open the System Folder on your hard drive, and then open the Control Strip Modules folder. Drag the desired module icon outside the Control Strip Modules folder and restart your iMac.

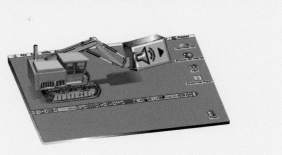

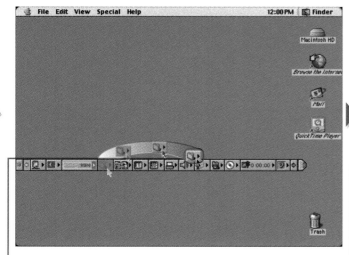

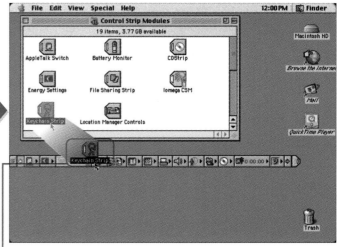

■ To move the items in the Control Strip, hold down the Option key and drag an item to its new position. Then release the Option key and mouse button.

■ You can add a Control Strip module by dragging the module to the Control Strip.

USING SLEEP MODE

Your iMac features a power-saving *sleep mode,* in which the iMac monitor and hard drive automatically turn off after a certain amount of inactivity.

To wake your iMac from sleep mode, simply move the mouse or press any key.

USING SLEEP MODE

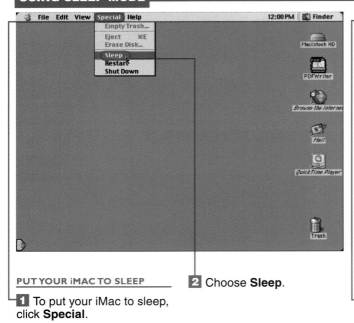

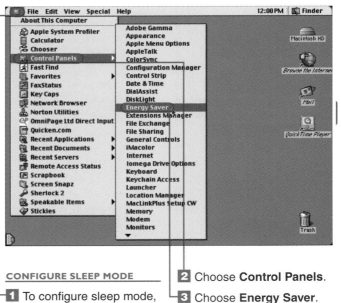

PUT YOUR iMAC TO SLEEP

1 To put your iMac to sleep, click **Special**.

2 Choose **Sleep**.

CONFIGURE SLEEP MODE

1 To configure sleep mode, click the Apple Menu.

2 Choose **Control Panels**.

3 Choose **Energy Saver**.

Why use sleep mode?

Allowing your iMac to automatically go into sleep mode is often more convenient than shutting your iMac down completely, because it takes less time for your computer to start up again from sleep mode.

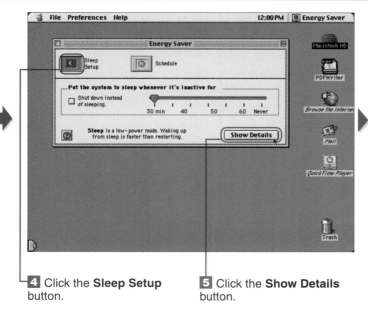

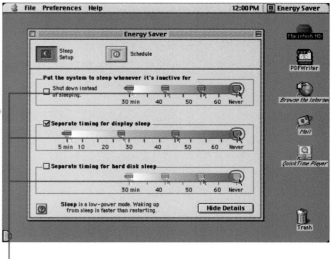

4 Click the **Sleep Setup** button.

5 Click the **Show Details** button.

6 To disable automatic sleep mode, move all three slider controls to Never.

SHUT DOWN AND RESTART YOUR IMAC

Many programs require you to restart your iMac after you install them. Restarting your iMac is essentially the same as turning it off and then turning it back on.

You should shut down your iMac whenever you plan to not use it for quite a while.

SHUT DOWN AND RESTART YOUR IMAC

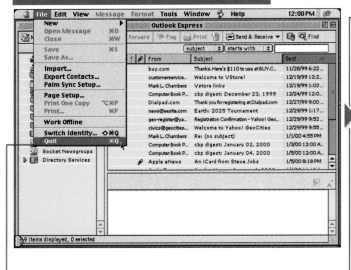

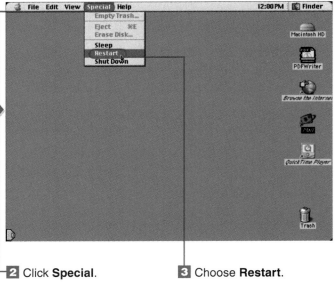

RESTART YOUR iMAC

1 To restart your iMac, close down any open applications and save any open documents.

2 Click **Special**.

3 Choose **Restart**.

What happens if I just turn off my iMac without shutting down?

Shutting down your computer without following Steps 3 and 4 below may result in disk errors and corrupted data. (You should always shut down your computer before you move it, too.)

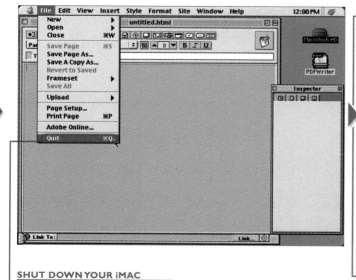

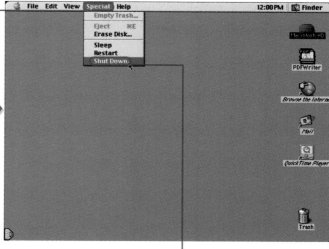

SHUT DOWN YOUR iMAC

1 To shut down your iMac, close down any open applications and save any open documents.

2 Click **Special**.

3 Choose **Shut Down**.

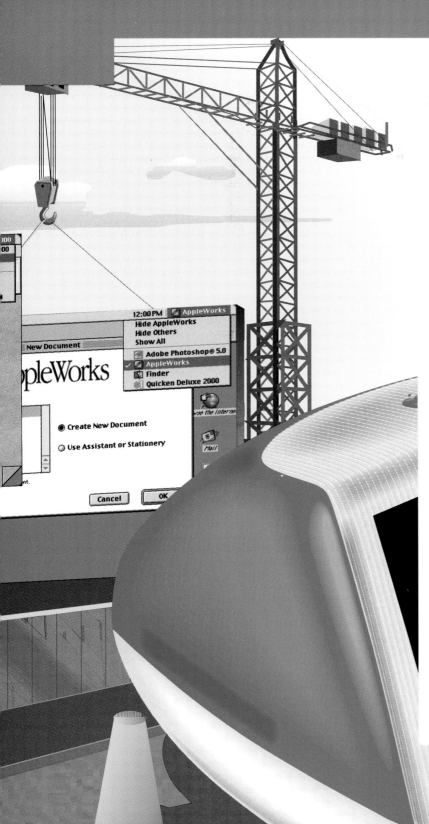

CHAPTER 3

Running and Switching Programs

Software programs make it so that you can do stuff with your iMac. This chapter gives you the basics on how to launch and quit programs.

RUN DESKTOP PROGRAMS AND ALIASES

An *alias* is an
icon that acts as
a shortcut to a
program, folder,
file, or drive.

RUN DESKTOP PROGRAMS AND ALIASES

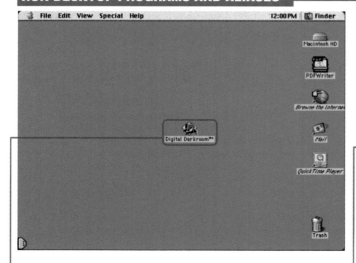

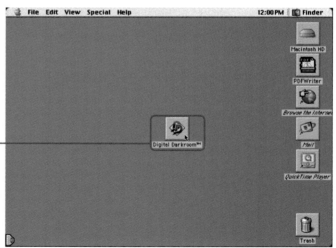

**RUN A PROGRAM
FROM THE DESKTOP**

1 To run a program from
your desktop, move the
mouse cursor over the
program icon and double-
click.

**RUN A PROGRAM
IN BUTTON VIEW**

1 If you've set your View
mode to display programs
and files as Buttons, only
a single click is required.

How can I tell a program from an alias?

Although an alias appears with the same icon as the actual program, it carries an italic description and a small curved arrow called a *badge*.

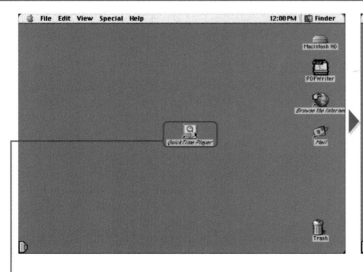

**RUN A PROGRAM
FROM AN ALIAS**

■ To run a program from an alias, double-click the alias icon.

Note: The names of aliases appear in italics.

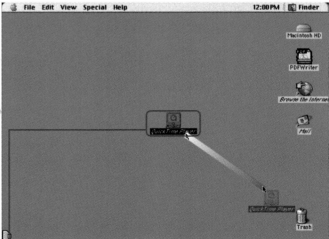

■ To delete an alias, drag it to the Trash. Only the alias is deleted; the original icon and program remain.

RUN A PROGRAM FROM YOUR HARD DRIVE

If you want to run a program that's stored on your hard drive but not visible on your desktop, you need to launch it from your hard drive.

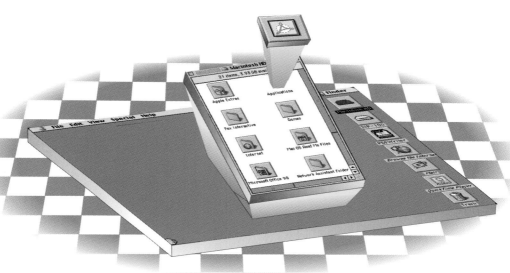

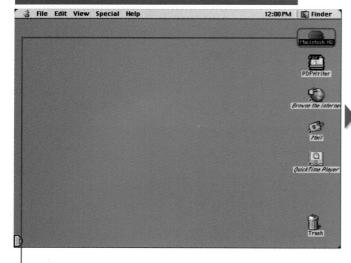

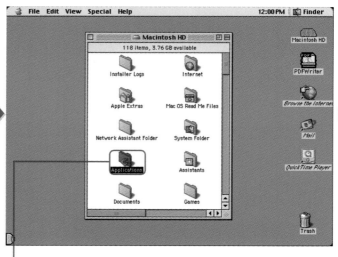

1 Double-click your hard drive icon to open it.

2 If the program icon is stored in a folder, double-click the folder to open it.

3 If the program is stored within multiple folders, repeat Step 2 as necessary.

I can't find a particular program — how can I locate it on my hard drive?

By using Sherlock 2, you can search for programs, files, folders, and so on. See Chapter 11 for details on using it.

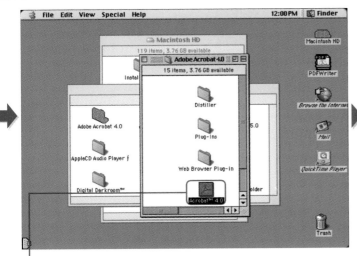

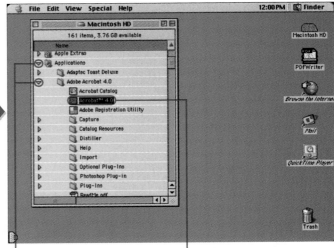

4 After the desired program icon appears, double-click it to run it.

5 If you're using List mode, click the triangle next to each folder to open it until the desired program appears.

6 Double-click the program name to run it.

RUN A PROGRAM FROM A CD-ROM OR DVD-ROM

You can run programs directly from a CD-ROM or DVD-ROM disc.

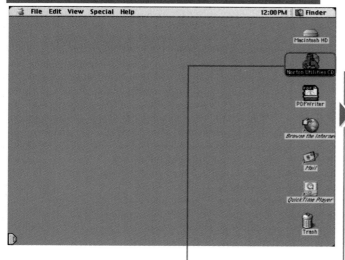

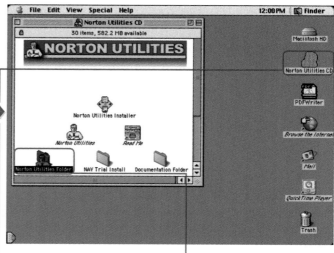

1 Insert the disc into your CD-ROM or DVD-ROM drive.

■ The disc appears on your desktop.

2 Double-click the disc's icon to display its contents.

3 If the program icon is stored in a folder, double-click the folder to open it.

4 If the program is stored within multiple folders, repeat Step 3 as necessary.

My iMac tells me that the CD-ROM I just loaded can't be read and needs to be formatted. What's wrong?

Make sure that you haven't loaded a CD-ROM meant for a Windows PC by mistake.

The disc may be badly scratched or smudged. If it is, clean it with a CD-ROM disc cleaner.

Finally, make sure that the printed side of the CD-ROM is facing up when you load it into your iMac drive.

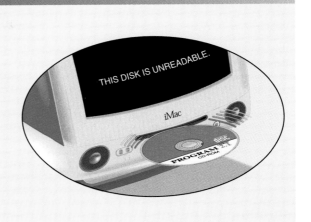

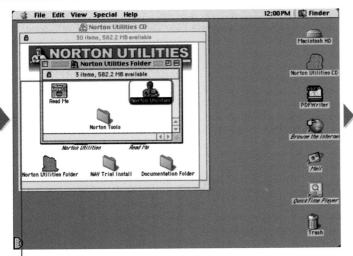

5 After the desired program icon appears, double-click it.

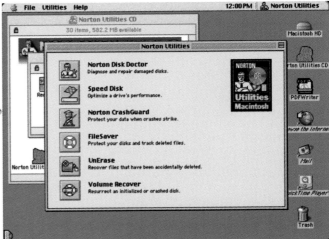

■ The program launches.

SWITCH PROGRAMS WITH THE APPLICATION MENU

Although your iMac can run many programs at once, only a single program can be *active* at once. The Application menu allows you to switch between programs that are already running.

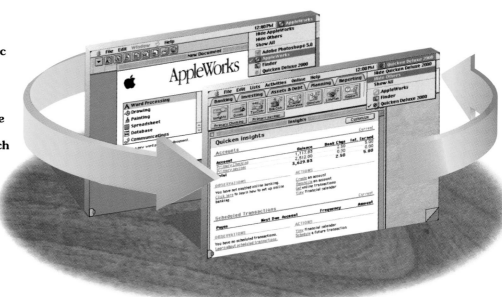

SWITCH PROGRAMS WITH THE APPLICATION MENU

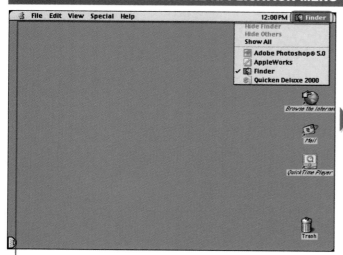

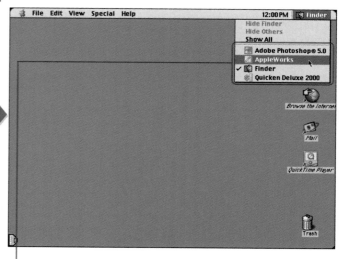

1 Display the Application Menu by clicking on the text label in the upper-right corner of the menu bar.

■ The text label always shows the currently active program.

2 Click the name of the program that you want to activate.

I'm running a program, but it doesn't show on the screen. Where is it?

If the program appears in the Application Menu, the program is hidden or collapsed. Click the entry in the Application menu and the program reappears.

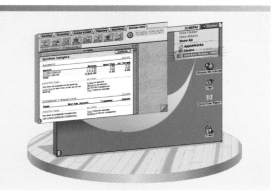

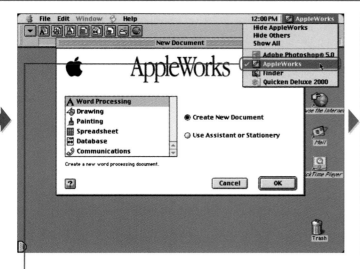

■ A checkmark (✓) appears next to the program's name in the Application menu, indicating that it is now active.

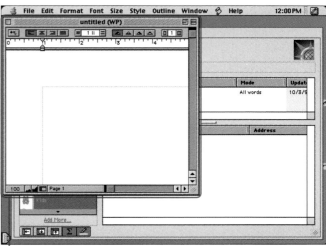

3 You can also make a program active by clicking once within the borders of a program's window.

CREATE A NEW ALIAS

You can create an alias
for a program icon using
the menu system.

CREATE A NEW ALIAS

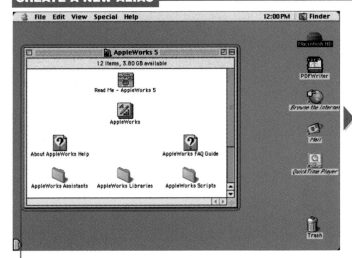

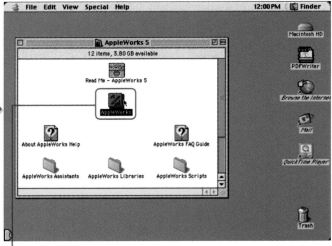

1 Navigate to the program's
icon – if it's not on the
desktop, locate it on your
hard drive.

2 Select the desired icon.

*Note: If you are viewing files As
Buttons, you may find it easier to
switch to the As Icons View mode.*

Can I create more than one alias for a program?

Yes. For example, you can place one on your desktop and another in your Applications folder to save you time.

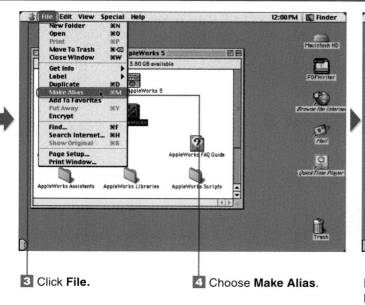

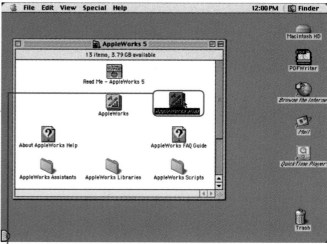

3 Click **File.**

4 Choose **Make Alias**.

■ The alias icon for your program appears.

5 Drag the new alias icon to the desired location and release the mouse button to move it.

CREATE A FLOATING APPLICATION SWITCHER

The *Application Switcher* is a convenient way to run several programs at once without using the Application menu.

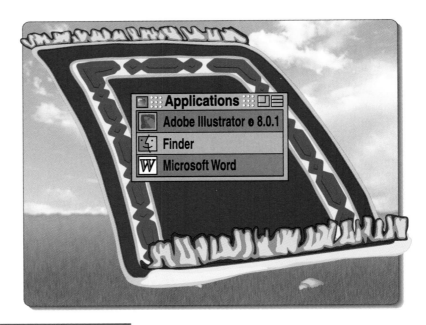

CREATE A FLOATING APPLICATION SWITCHER

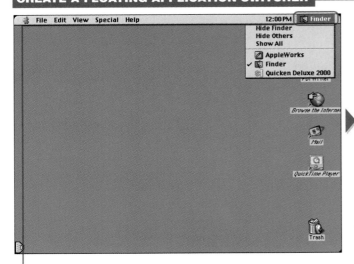

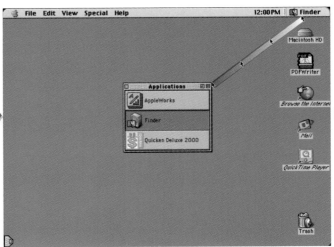

1 Display the Application Menu by clicking on the text label in the upper-right corner of the menu bar.

2 Click on the text label and drag the mouse below the bottom of the Application menu. An outline of a window appears.

Can I shrink the Application Switcher?

Click the Zoom box in the corner of the Switcher to display only the program icons. To display smaller icons and save even more space, press and hold down the Option key while you click the Zoom box.

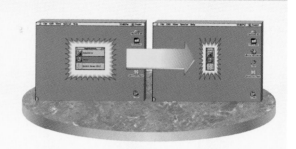

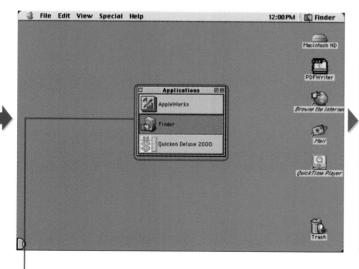

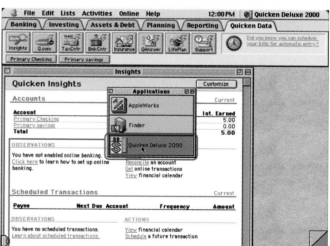

3 Drag the outline onto your desktop and release the button to create the Application Switcher.

4 To activate a different program, click the desired program in the Application Switcher.

HIDE AND RESIZE WINDOWS

You can *hide* the active window (which removes the entire window completely from your desktop), *resize* it, or *maximize* it.

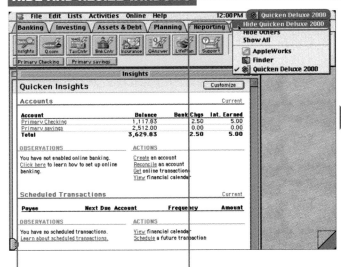

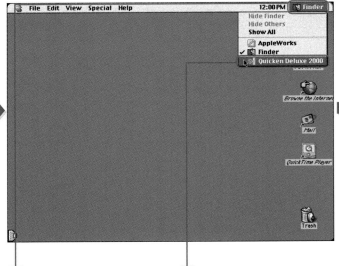

1 To hide the active program, click the Application menu by clicking in the upper-right corner of the menu bar.

2 Select the **Hide** menu item for the program.

3 To switch back to the hidden program, click the Application menu.

4 Click the hidden program.

**Why are some program icons
grayed out in the Application
menu?**

When a program's icon is grayed
out, the program is currently
hidden.

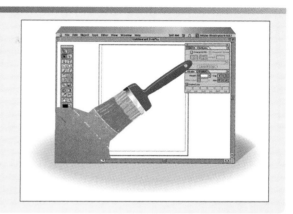

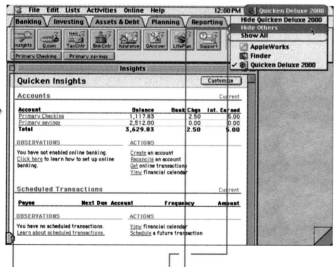

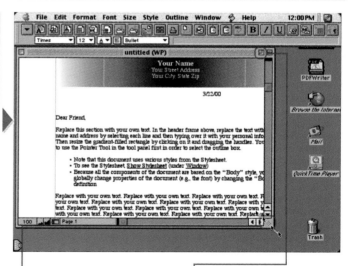

5 To hide all inactive
program windows, click
the Application menu.

6 Choose **Hide Others**.

7 To return all windows
to their original positions,
choose **Show All**.

8 Resize the active window
by dragging the Size box in
or out.

9 Expand the active
program window to its
maximum size by holding
down the Option key and
clicking on the Zoom box.

DISPLAY ALIAS AND PROGRAM INFORMATION

You can display or
change information
about a file, a program,
or an alias.

DISPLAY ALIAS AND PROGRAM INFORMATION

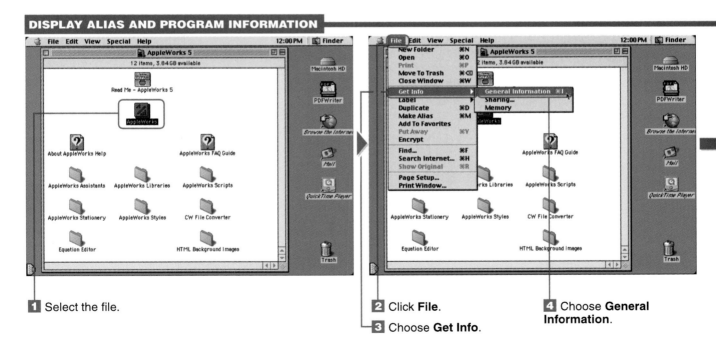

1 Select the file.

2 Click **File**.

3 Choose **Get Info**.

4 Choose **General Information**.

**What other data can I find in the
Info window?**

What you see depends on the
type of file you have selected —
for example, programs also display
Sharing and Memory information.

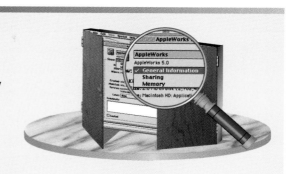

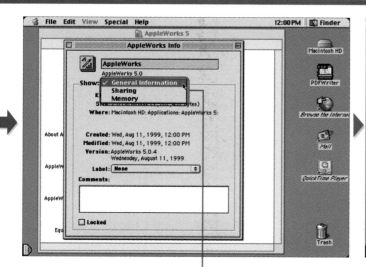

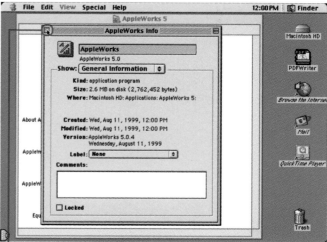

■ The Info window appears.

5 To display additional
information, click on the
Show drop-down list box and
select the desired
information.

6 Click on the Close box to
close the Info window.

USE AND CUSTOMIZE THE LAUNCHER

The Mac OS includes
a program called the
Launcher, which displays
icons as buttons; with
the Launcher, you can
conveniently click once
on a program to run it.

USE AND CUSTOMIZE THE LAUNCHER

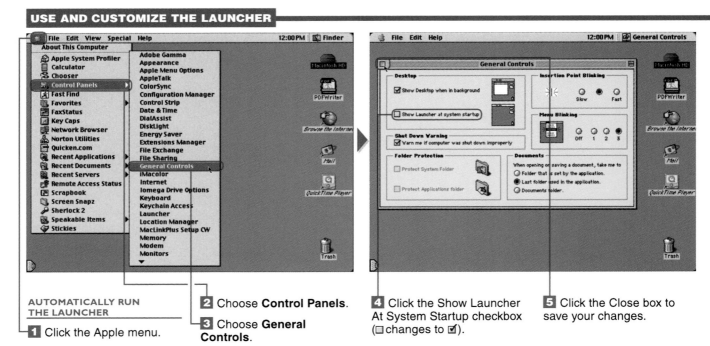

**AUTOMATICALLY RUN
THE LAUNCHER**

1 Click the Apple menu.

2 Choose **Control Panels**.

3 Choose **General Controls**.

4 Click the Show Launcher At System Startup checkbox (□ changes to ☑).

5 Click the Close box to save your changes.

How can I create a new folder within the Launcher?

Open the System folder and then open the Launcher Items folder. Click **File** and choose **New Folder.** Press and hold the Option key and press 8. Type the name of the folder and press the Return key.

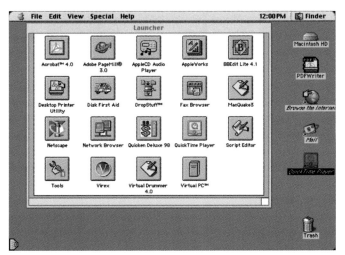

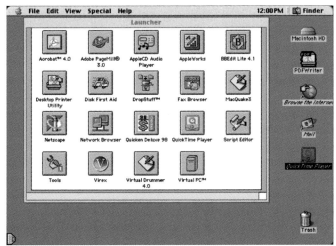

**ADD ITEMS TO
THE LAUNCHER**

1 To add an icon to the Launcher, drag it into the Launcher window.

**REMOVE ITEMS FROM
THE LAUNCHER**

1 To remove an icon from the Launcher, hold down the Option key and drag the icon anywhere but the desktop.

QUIT PROGRAMS

Your iMac will run faster and more efficiently if you quit a program after you finish using it.

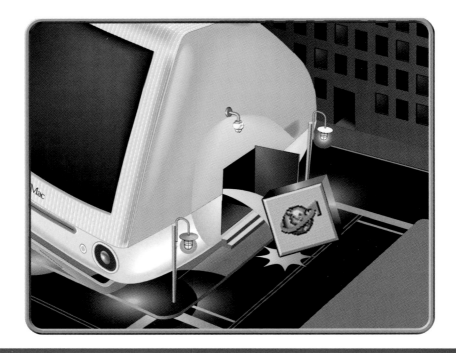

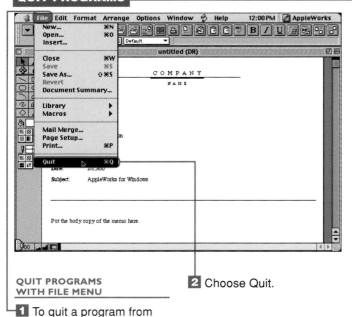

**QUIT PROGRAMS
WITH FILE MENU**

1 To quit a program from the menu bar, click **File**.

2 Choose Quit.

**QUIT USING KEYBOARD
SHORTCUTS**

1 To exit most programs from the keyboard, press and hold the ⌘ key and press Q.

When I close a program window, the program doesn't quit. Why?

Closing a program window under Mac OS may not necessarily quit the program. Programs such as AppleWorks, for example, stay running even if you close all the program's windows.

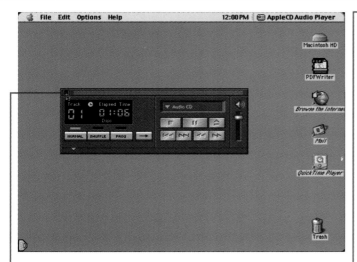

QUIT USING CLOSE BOX

1 Some programs may also quit if you close their window.

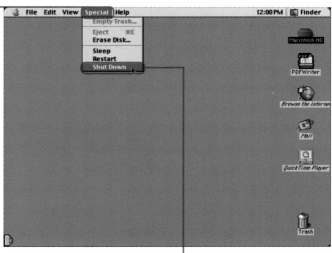

QUIT ALL PROGRAMS

1 To quit all running programs and shut down your iMac, click **Special**.

2 Choose **Shut Down**.

CLOSE WINDOWS

Closing windows helps reduce clutter on your desktop.

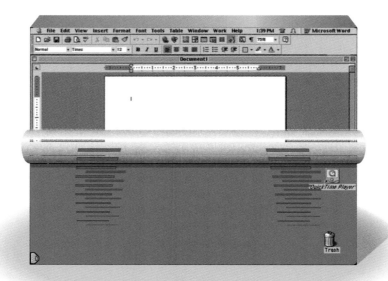

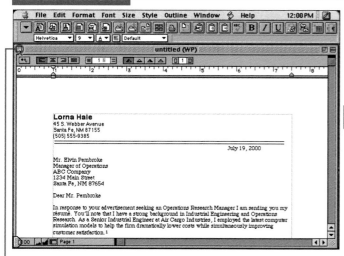

1 To close the active window, click the Close box.

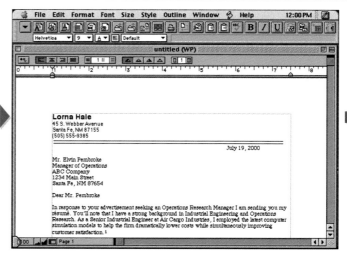

2 To close the active window from the keyboard, press and hold the ⌘ key and press W.

When I try to close a program, why do I get a prompt about saving my document.

If you have not saved your work and you try to close a program, the program prompts you to save to make sure that you don't accidentally lose your work.

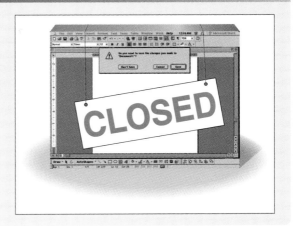

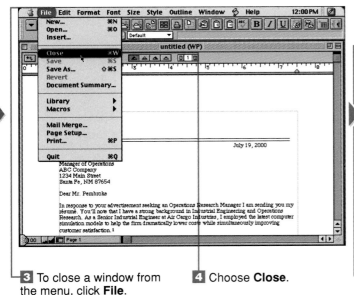

3 To close a window from the menu, click **File**.

4 Choose **Close**.

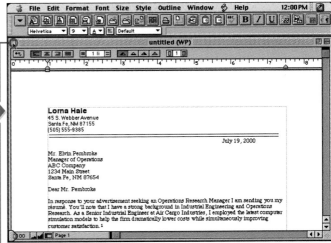

5 To close all open disk and folder windows for a program (whether they are active or not), hold down the Option key while you click the Close box.

WORK WITH RECENT PROGRAMS AND DOCUMENTS

From the Apple menu, you can quickly run recently used programs and open recently used documents.

WORK WITH RECENT PROGRAMS AND DOCUMENTS

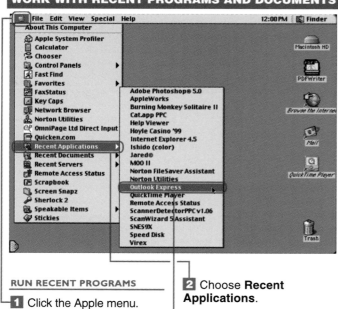

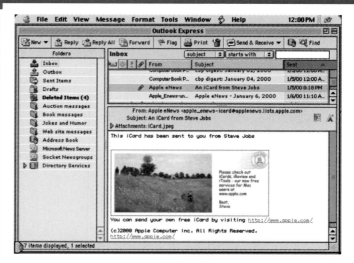

RUN RECENT PROGRAMS

1 Click the Apple menu.

2 Choose **Recent Applications**.

3 Choose the program you want to use.

■ The program appears.

**What actions add entries to the
Recent Applications and Recent
Documents menu?**

Whenever you run a program, it is
added to the Recent Applications
menu. Whenever you save, edit, or
create a document, it is added to
the Recent Documents menu.

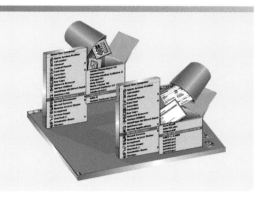

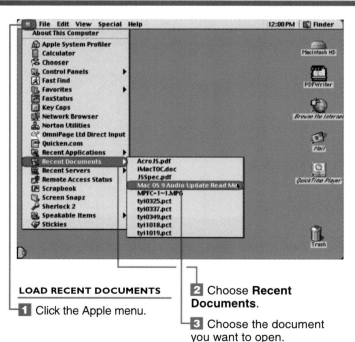

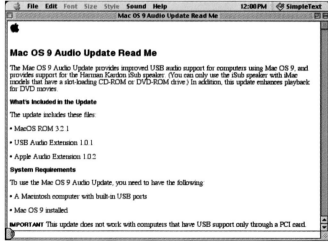

Mac OS 9 Audio Update Read Me

The Mac OS 9 Audio Update provides improved USB audio support for computers using Mac OS 9, and provides support for the Harman Kardon iSub speaker. (You can only use the iSub speaker with iMac models that have a slot-loading CD-ROM or DVD-ROM drive.) In addition, this update enhances playback for DVD movies.

What's Included in the Update

The update includes these files:

• MacOS ROM 3.2.1

• USB Audio Extension 1.0.1

• Apple Audio Extension 1.0.2

System Requirements

To use the Mac OS 9 Audio Update, you need to have the following:

• A Macintosh computer with built-in USB ports

• Mac OS 9 installed

IMPORTANT This update does not work with computers that have USB support only through a PCI card.

LOAD RECENT DOCUMENTS

1 Click the Apple menu.

2 Choose **Recent
Documents**.

3 Choose the document
you want to open.

■ The document appears.

*Note: iMac automatically launches
the appropriate program to load
your document.*

CHAPTER 4

Working with Files

You spend most of your time working with program files and documents. This chapter shows you how to manage your files in the Mac OS.

You can easily
change the name
of a disk, file, or
folder.

Date: Saturday, July 15, 2000
Time: 10:30 AM - 6:00 PM
Venue: Garden Gate Park

All employees are invited to bring their families out for a fun-filled day at the park. There will be plenty of food and lots of ... and activities for the whole

RENAME ITEMS

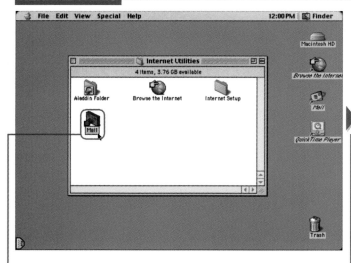

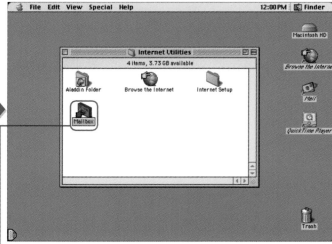

1 Click the filename under or beside the icon.

■ The current name is highlighted.

2 Type in the new filename and press Return.

Can I name my files whatever I want?

You can use any alphanumeric character in your filenames, and they can contain spaces. However, a filename can't be more than 31 characters long, and it can't contain any colons; a colon is automatically changed into a dash as you type it.

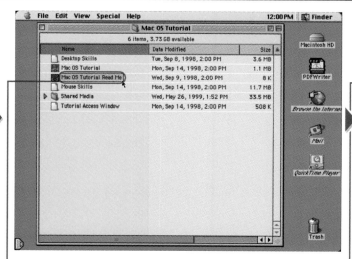

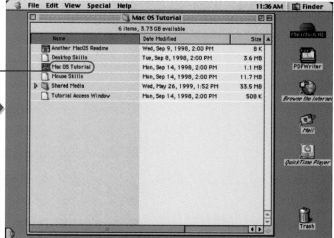

3 To change the name of a file in List view, click the filename in the list.

■ The current name is highlighted.

4 Type in the new filename and press Return.

■ The new name appears next to the icon.

LOCK FILES

If a file is locked, you can't change or delete the file, which can help prevent accidental changes or deletions. You can only open it and copy the file.

LOCK FILES

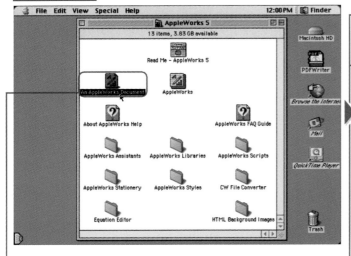

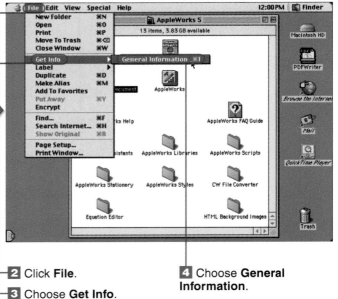

1 Click the icon to highlight it.

2 Click **File**.

3 Choose **Get Info**.

4 Choose **General Information**.

Working with
Files 4

How can I unlock a file?

To unlock a file so that you can edit it or delete it, follow the steps in this section, and click the Locked check box to uncheck it.

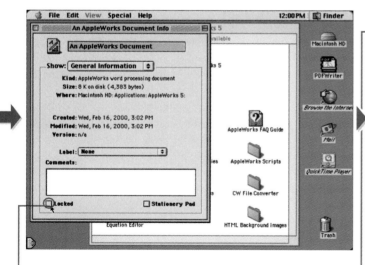

5 Click the Locked check box.

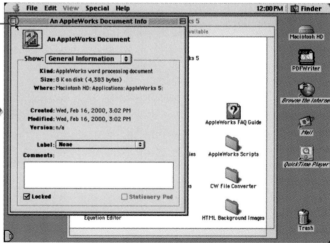

6 Click the Close box to save your changes.

USING LABELS AND COLORS

You can assign a label and color to a file to help identify and organize data.

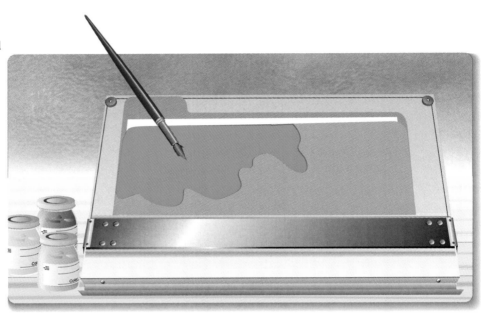

USING LABELS AND COLORS

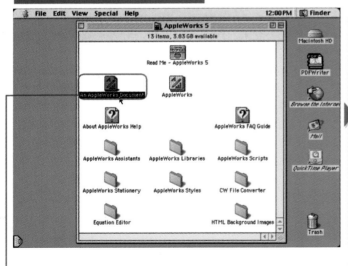

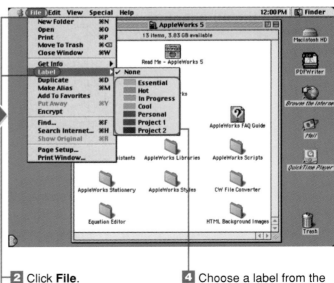

ADD A LABEL

1 Click the icon to select it.

2 Click **File**.

3 Choose **Label**.

4 Choose a label from the submenu.

Can I apply labels to folders as well?

Yes. Labels enable you to quickly organize your files and folders by project, by deadline, or by importance.

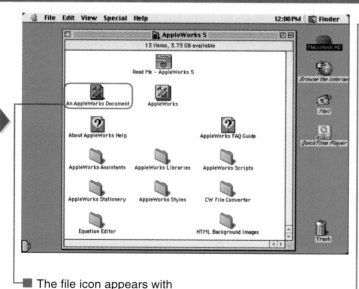

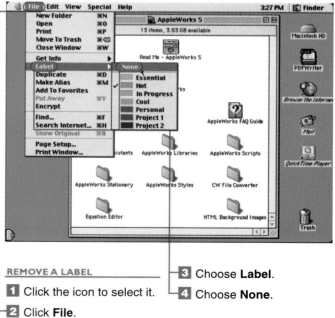

■ The file icon appears with its new color.

REMOVE A LABEL

1 Click the icon to select it.

2 Click **File**.

3 Choose **Label**.

4 Choose **None**.

EDIT LABELS

You can edit the default
labels that come on your
iMac to make your own
labels.

You can have only seven
labels at a time.

EDIT LABELS

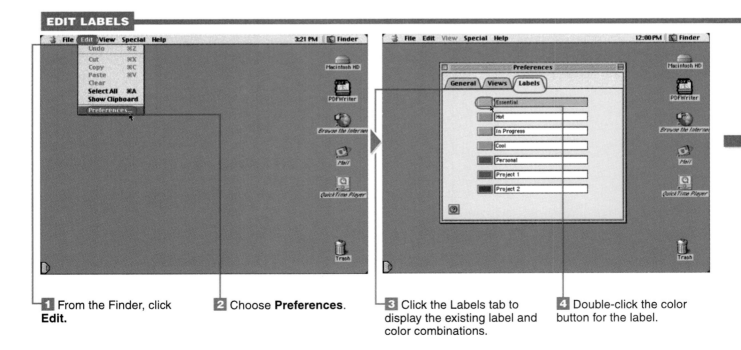

1 From the Finder, click
Edit.

2 Choose **Preferences**.

3 Click the Labels tab to
display the existing label and
color combinations.

4 Double-click the color
button for the label.

I want to set an exact color for a label. How can I do this?

To enter specific red/green/blue values for a color or make precise changes to the hue, saturation, and brightness values, display the Color Picker, click within the fields, and type the values.

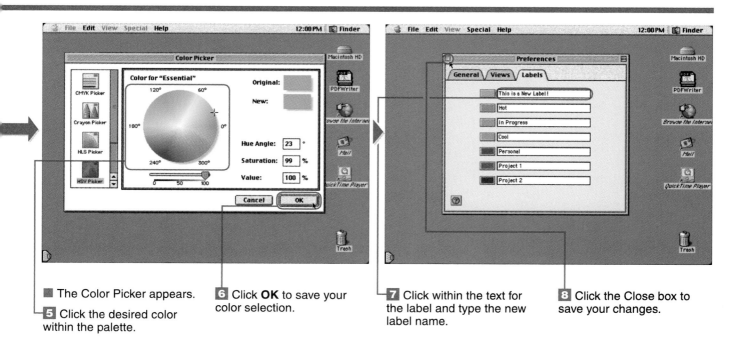

■ The Color Picker appears.

5 Click the desired color within the palette.

6 Click **OK** to save your color selection.

7 Click within the text for the label and type the new label name.

8 Click the Close box to save your changes.

VIEW LIST FILES BY LABEL

You can organize your important files by grouping them by label.

VIEW LIST FILES BY LABEL

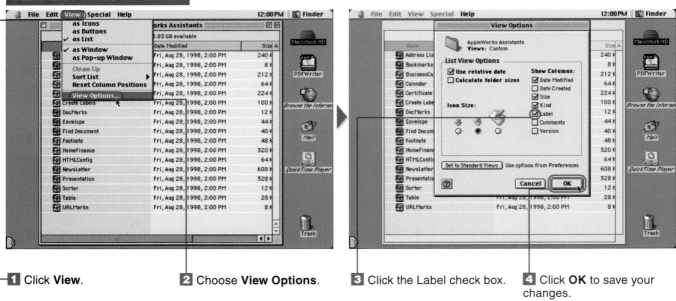

1 Click **View**.

2 Choose **View Options**.

3 Click the Label check box.

4 Click **OK** to save your changes.

Can I move all files with the same label?

Yes. View your files by label and select them as a group.

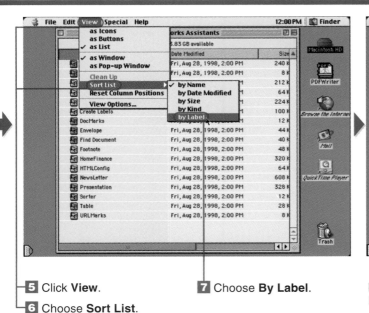

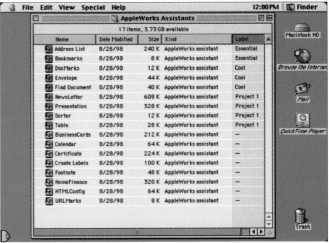

5 Click **View**.

6 Choose **Sort List**.

7 Choose **By Label**.

■ The files appear sorted by label.

REPLACE A FILE'S ICON

You can replace a file's icon with another icon. First, you make a copy of the new icon you want to use.

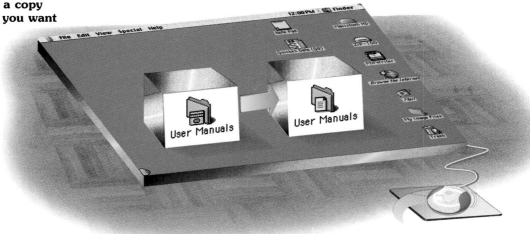

REPLACE A FILE'S ICON

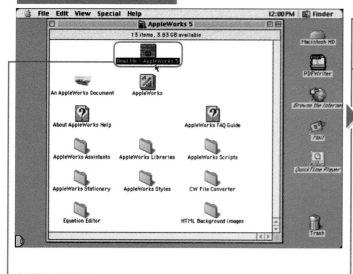

COPY AN ICON

1 Click the icon of the file you want to copy.

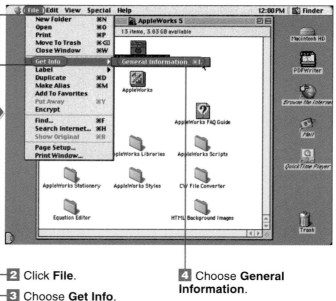

2 Click **File**.

3 Choose **Get Info**.

4 Choose **General Information**.

I can't replace the icon. Why?

Check to make sure that the file isn't locked, that the file isn't read-only, and that the file isn't currently being used.

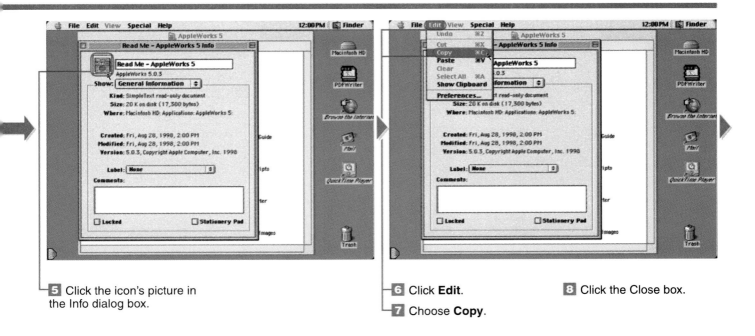

5 Click the icon's picture in the Info dialog box.

6 Click **Edit**.

7 Choose **Copy**.

8 Click the Close box.

CONTINUED

REPLACE A FILE'S ICON

After you copy the new icon image, you need to paste it over the old icon.

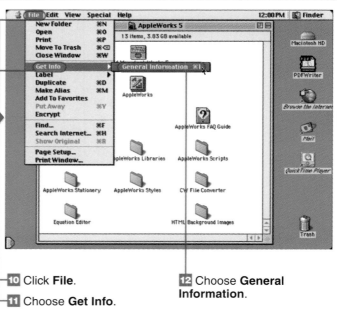

REPLACE A FILE'S ICON

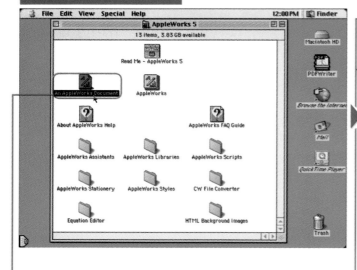

PASTE AN ICON

9 Click the icon you want to change to select it.

10 Click **File**.

11 Choose **Get Info**.

12 Choose **General Information**.

The Paste command is disabled when I try to add the image. Why?

If the Paste menu item is disabled, you haven't correctly copied the image or the icon can't be changed.

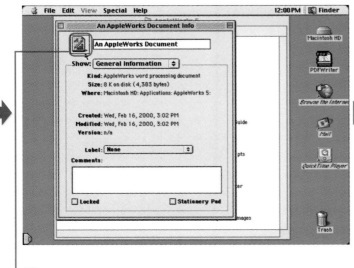

13 Click the icon's picture in the Info dialog box.

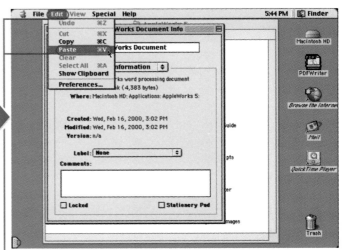

14 Click **Edit**.

15 Choose **Paste**.

16 Click the Close box to save your change.

■ After you close the Info box, you can see the new icon.

LOAD A CD-ROM OR DVD

Most applications you
install on your iMac are
stored on CD-ROMs —
and some iMacs can also
read DVD discs and play
DVD movies.

*Note: CD-ROMs and
DVDs are read-only;
you can't edit
documents or write
data to them*

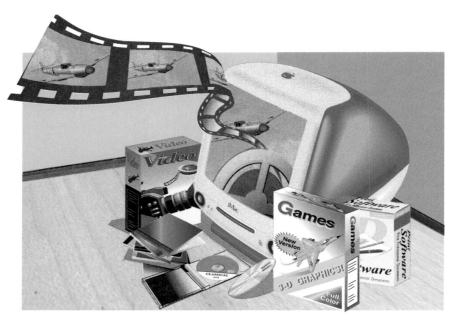

LOAD A CD-ROM OR DVD

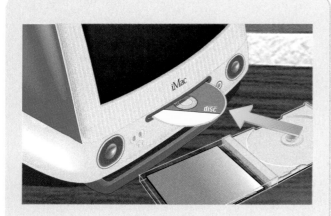

1 Push the disc into your iMac's drive slot with the
label side facing up.

2 Your iMac should automatically display the
contents of the disc.

*Note: If not, then just double-click the
CD-ROM's icon.*

**My iMac doesn't have a disc slot.
How do I load a disc?**

Older iMacs use CD-ROM drives
with trays. To eject the tray and
load the disc, press the button on
the front of the drive.

3 Double-click the application or document
icon to run the program.

4 When you're finished with the disc, drag the
disc icon to the Trash.

■ The CD-ROM ejects.

PLAY A MUSIC CD

You can play music CDs
with the AppleCD Audio
Player, turning your iMac
into a stereo system.

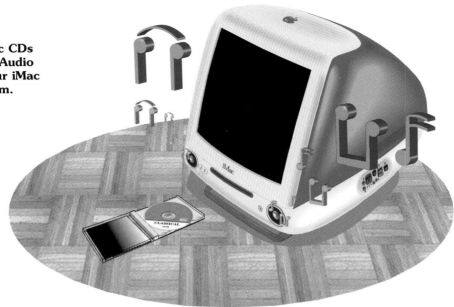

PLAY A MUSIC CD

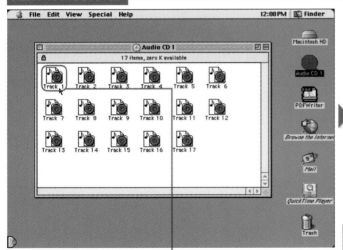

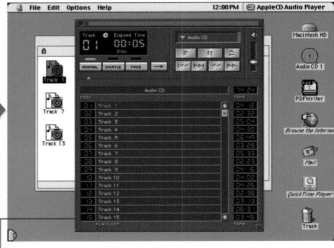

PLAY CDS FROM THE DESKTOP

1 Load a music CD into
your drive as shown in
section "Load a CD-ROM
or DVD."

2 Double-click the audio
CD icon on the desktop.

■ The Audio CD window
appears showing the tracks
on the disc.

3 Double-click the track you
want to hear.

■ The AppleCD Audio
Player automatically
launches.

What if I don't hear any music when I play an audio CD?

Make sure that the speaker volume is set correctly and that the audio hasn't been muted. You can find these controls on the Sound Control Panel.

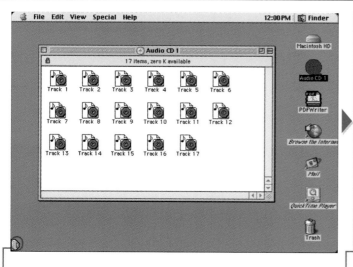

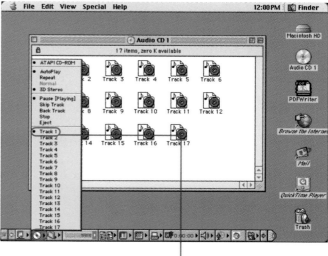

PLAY CDS FROM THE CONTROL STRIP

1 Click the Control Strip tab.

2 Click the CD Control Strip button.

3 Choose the track you want to hear.

LOAD PC FILES

By assigning Macintosh
applications to certain
types of PC files, your
iMac can load files
created on a DOS or
Windows PC.

Depending on the
applications that you've
loaded, some PC files
will be automatically
recognized by your
iMac.

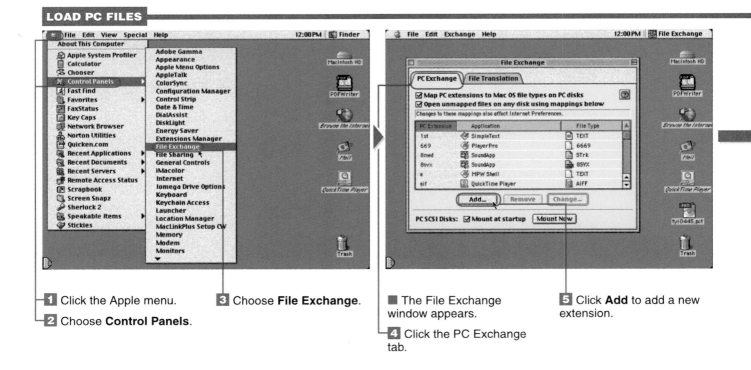

■1 Click the Apple menu.

■2 Choose **Control Panels**.

■3 Choose **File Exchange**.

■ The File Exchange
window appears.

■4 Click the PC Exchange
tab.

■5 Click **Add** to add a new
extension.

What is a file extension?

A file extension is a series of up to four letters that follow the period in a filename. The Mac OS usually hides file extensions for your convenience. The extension tells you which program created and, therefore, will open a file.

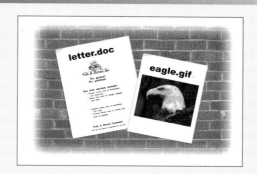

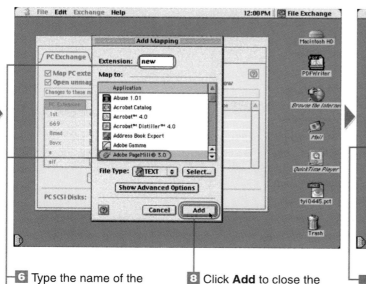

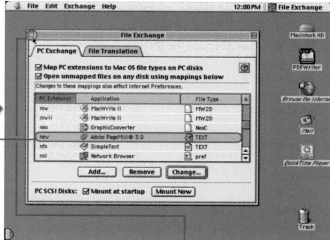

6 Type the name of the extension you want to add.

7 Choose the application that you want to automatically open this type of file.

8 Click **Add** to close the dialog box and save your changes.

■ The new extension appears in the list on the File Exchange window.

9 Click the Close box to save your changes.

EMPTY AND RESTORE FILES FROM THE TRASH

Emptying the Trash is a simple menu command away.

You can also restore a file in the Trash before you empty it.

EMPTY AND RESTORE FILES FROM THE TRASH

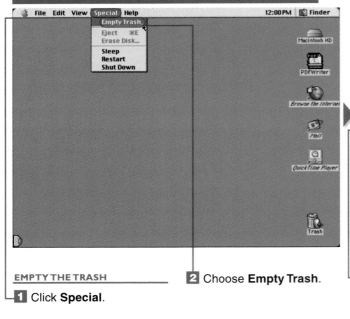

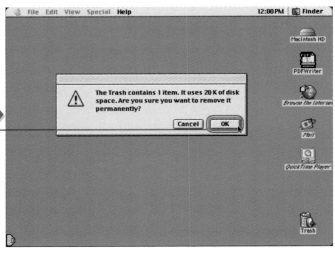

EMPTY THE TRASH

1 Click **Special**.

2 Choose **Empty Trash**.

3 Click **OK** to confirm that you do want to empty the Trash.

How can I turn off that annoying confirmation dialog box when I empty the Trash?

To turn off the warning dialog box, click once on the Trash icon to select it, then click **File** and choose **Get Info**. Disable the Warn before emptying check box, and click the Close box to save your changes.

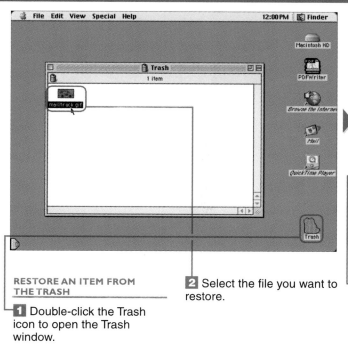
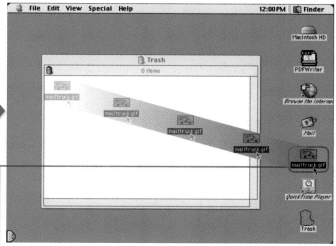

RESTORE AN ITEM FROM THE TRASH

1 Double-click the Trash icon to open the Trash window.

2 Select the file you want to restore.

3 Drag the selected file to your desktop or to another folder.

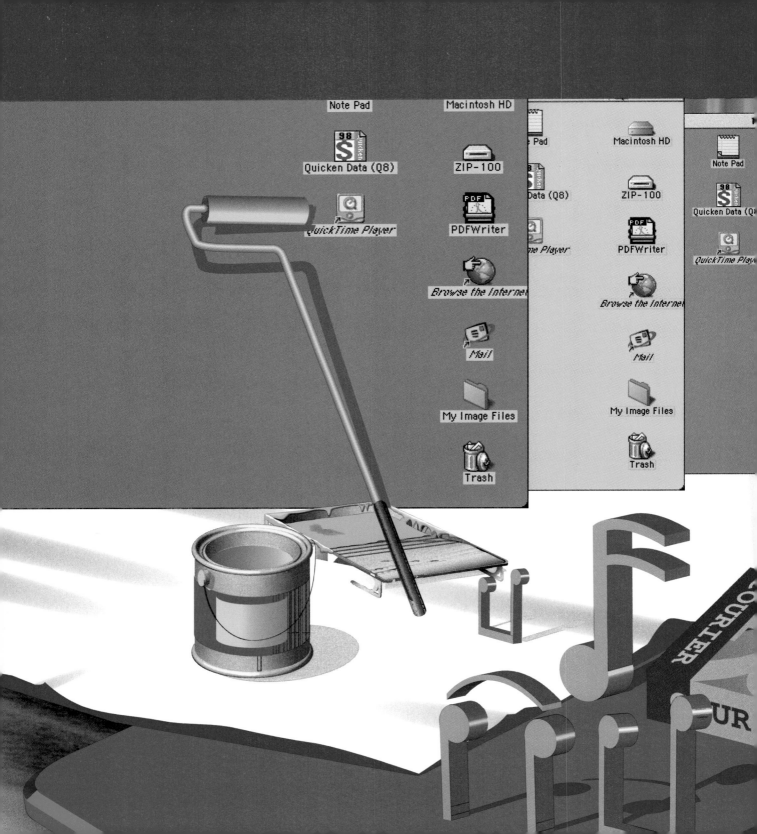

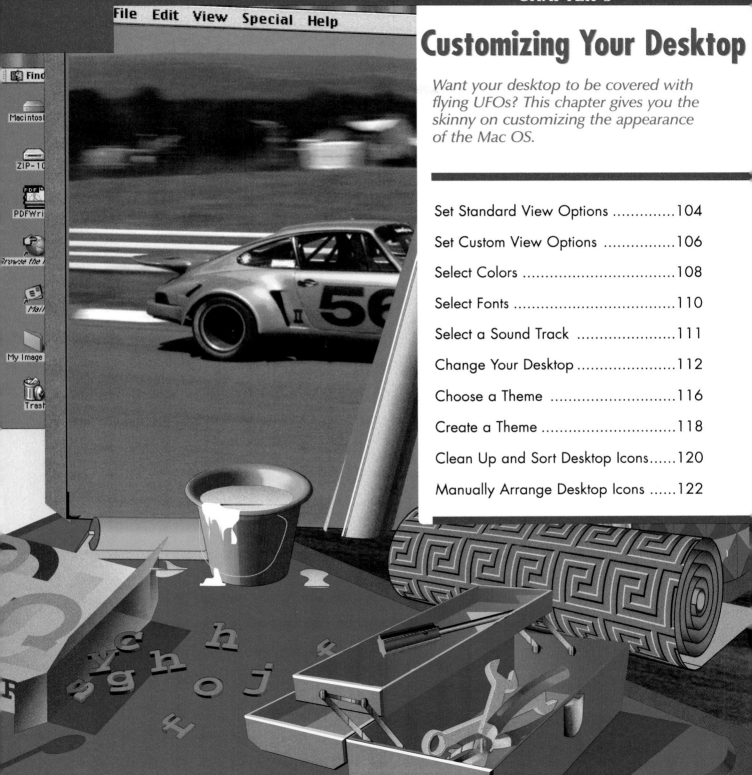

CHAPTER 5

Customizing Your Desktop

Want your desktop to be covered with flying UFOs? This chapter gives you the skinny on customizing the appearance of the Mac OS.

SET STANDARD VIEW OPTIONS

The Mac OS uses a set of standard view options that you can customize through the Finder. Every drive and folder window uses these options by default.

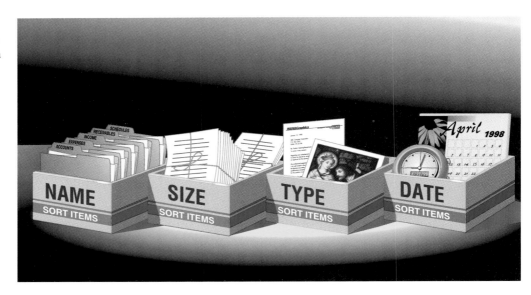

SET STANDARD VIEW OPTIONS

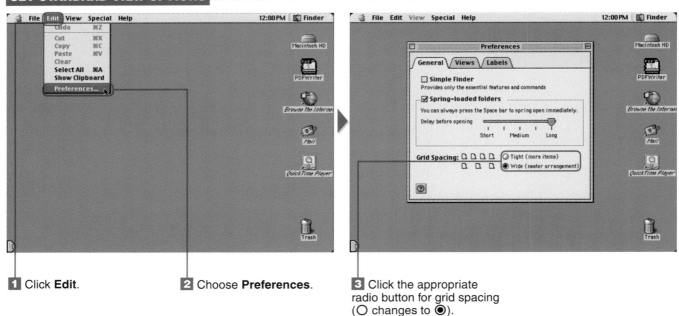

1 Click **Edit**.

2 Choose **Preferences**.

3 Click the appropriate radio button for grid spacing (○ changes to ◉).

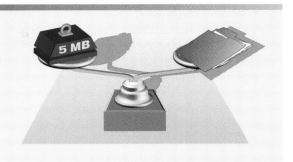

How can I display the total size of a folder's contents?

If you are using List viewing mode, display the standard view options for List mode and click the Calculate Folder Sizes check box.

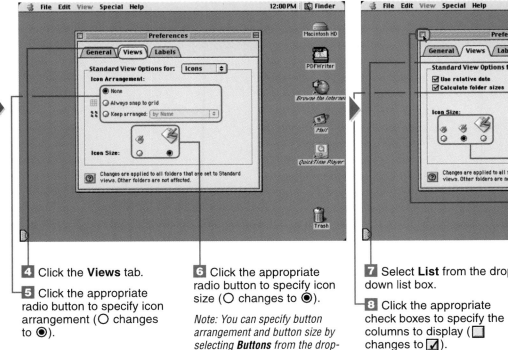

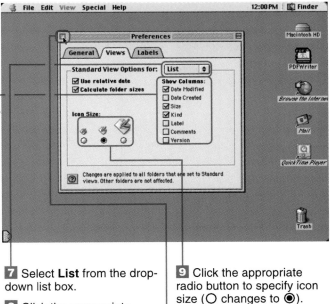

4 Click the **Views** tab.

5 Click the appropriate radio button to specify icon arrangement (○ changes to ●).

6 Click the appropriate radio button to specify icon size (○ changes to ●).

*Note: You can specify button arrangement and button size by selecting **Buttons** from the drop-down list.*

7 Select **List** from the drop-down list box.

8 Click the appropriate check boxes to specify the columns to display (☐ changes to ☑).

9 Click the appropriate radio button to specify icon size (○ changes to ●).

10 Click the Close box to save your changes.

SET CUSTOM VIEW OPTIONS

You can set custom view options for a specific folder or drive to override the standard view options.

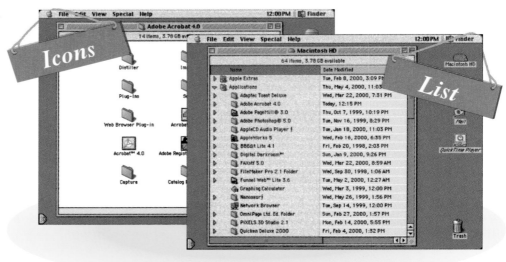

SET CUSTOM VIEW OPTIONS

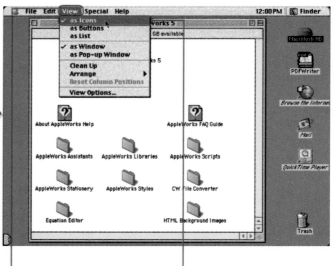

1 Open the drive or folder that you want to customize.

2 Click **View**.

3 Select a viewing mode by choosing **As Icons**, **As Buttons**, or **As List**.

**How can I return my folder or
drive to the Standard view?**

To return to the standard settings
for the current viewing mode, click
View and choose **View Options**.
Then click **Set To Standard Views**
and click **OK.**

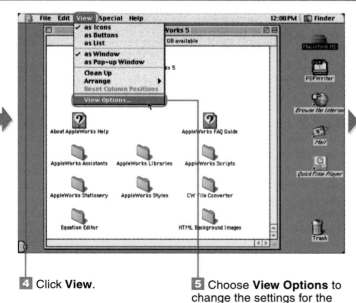

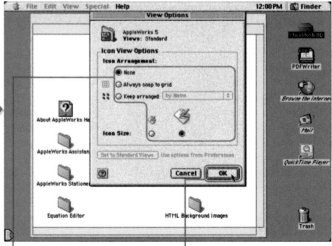

4 Click **View**.

5 Choose **View Options** to
change the settings for the
current viewing mode.

6 Click the appropriate
radio buttons to specify icon
arrangement and icon size
(○ changes to ◉)

7 Click **OK** to exit and save
your changes.

SELECT COLORS

Your iMac can display two different colors that you choose for several screen objects.

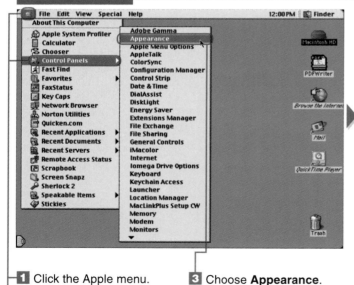

1 Click the Apple menu.

2 Choose **Control Panels**.

3 Choose **Appearance**.

4 Click the **Appearance** tab.

5 Click the Highlight Color drop-down list and click the desired color for highlights.

What is the difference between Highlight and Variation colors?

The *Highlight* color is used to highlight text during copy, delete, or edit operations. The *Variation* color is displayed for menu and window controls such as scroll bars and selected menu items.

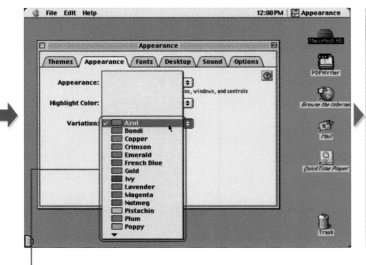

6 Click the Variation drop-down list and click the desired color for control variations.

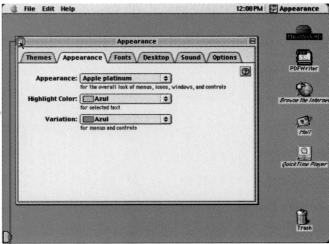

7 Click the Close box to save your changes.

SELECT FONTS

You can choose from three unique display fonts to use throughout the operating system.

SELECT FONTS

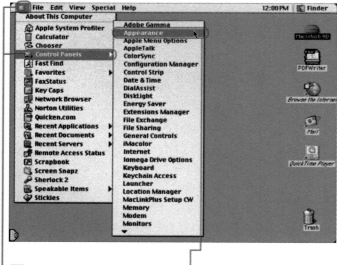

1 Click the Apple menu.

2 Choose **Control Panels**.

3 Choose **Appearance**.

4 Click the **Fonts** tab.

5 Click each of the font drop-down lists and choose the desired font for each.

6 Click the Size selector to choose a font size.

7 Click the Close box to save your changes.

SELECT A SOUND TRACK

A sound track is a set of
sound effects that play
when common system
events occur, such as
running programs or
opening and closing
windows.

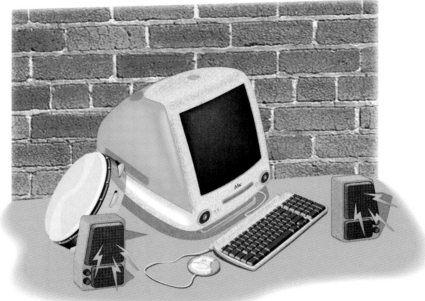

SELECT A SOUND TRACK

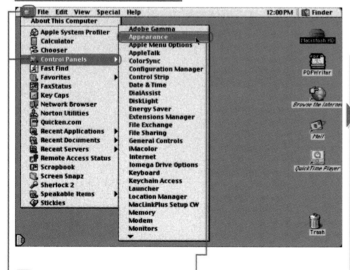

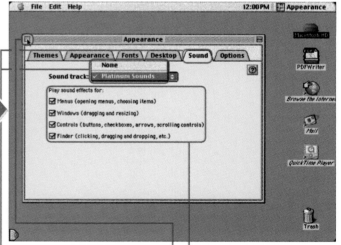

1 Click the Apple menu.

2 Choose **Control Panels**.

3 Choose **Appearance**.

4 Click the **Sound** tab.

5 Click the Sound track
drop-down list and choose
a sound track.

6 Click the appropriate
check boxes to turn on
sound effects (☐ changes
to ☑).

7 Click the Close box to
save your changes.

CHANGE YOUR DESKTOP

You can customize your
iMac desktop with
patterns or pictures.

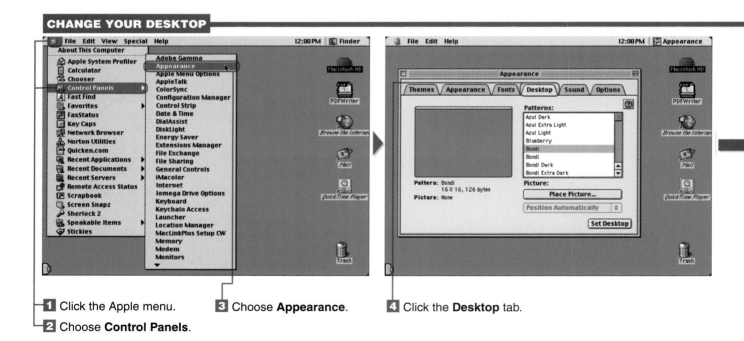

1 Click the Apple menu.

2 Choose **Control Panels**.

3 Choose **Appearance**.

4 Click the **Desktop** tab.

I chose the Fill Screen position setting, and the picture looks really strange on my desktop. What happened?

If you use the Fill Screen setting, an image that is smaller than the desktop will be expanded to fit, which may distort the image.

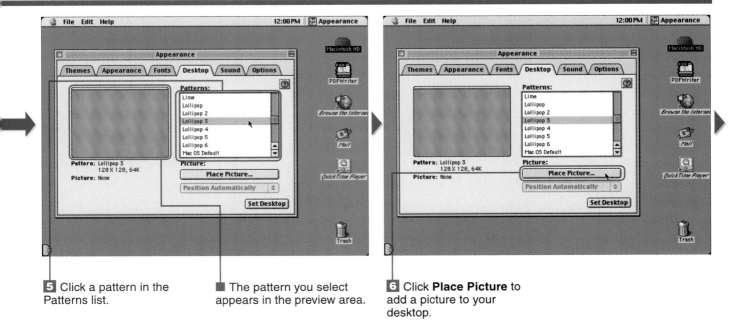

5 Click a pattern in the Patterns list.

■ The pattern you select appears in the preview area.

6 Click **Place Picture** to add a picture to your desktop.

CONTINUED

CHANGE YOUR DESKTOP

Your iMac offers several pictures to choose from.

CHANGE YOUR DESKTOP

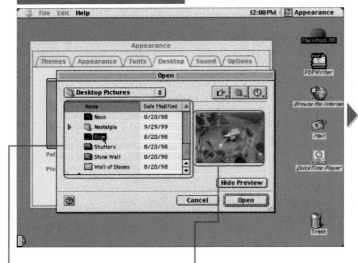

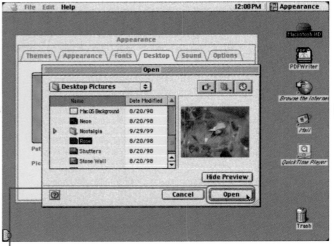

■ The Open dialog box appears.

7 Click a picture from the list.

■ The picture you select appears in the preview window.

8 Click **Open** to load the new picture.

**What does the Tile On Screen
option do?**

It fills your desktop in a tiled effect
with many small versions of the
selected picture.

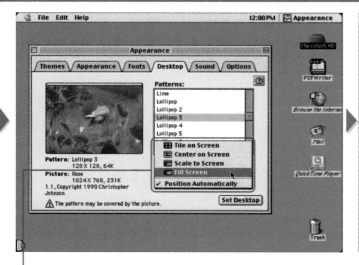

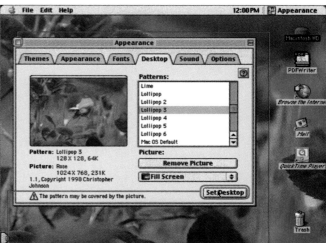

9 To specify the position of
the picture, click the desired
position from the drop-down
list.

10 To accept your changes,
click **Set Desktop**.

■ Your picture appears on
the desktop.

11 Click the Close box to
save your changes.

CHOOSE A THEME

By using a *theme,* you can choose a group of Appearance settings at once.

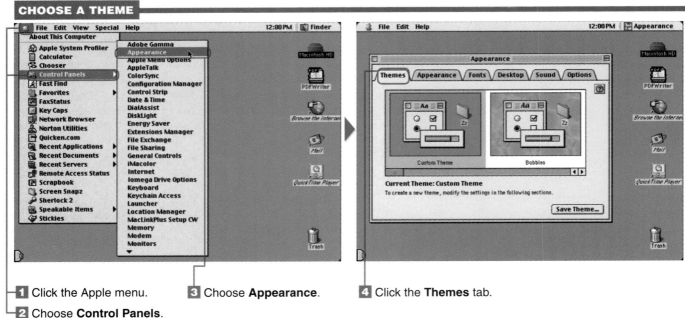

1 Click the Apple menu.

2 Choose **Control Panels**.

3 Choose **Appearance**.

4 Click the **Themes** tab.

What appearance elements make up a theme?

All of them! A theme sets the desktop pattern and picture, the fonts, the sound track, and the system colors.

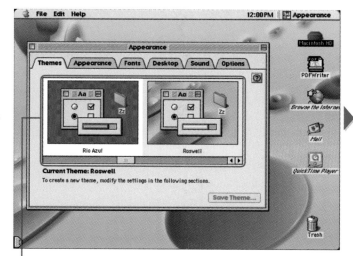

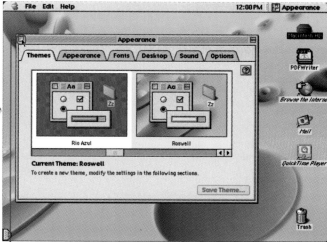

5 Scroll through the preview of each theme and click the preview that you want to see.

■ The new theme takes effect.

6 Click the Close box to exit and save your changes.

CREATE A THEME

You can configure a
custom appearance to
create your own theme.

CREATE A THEME

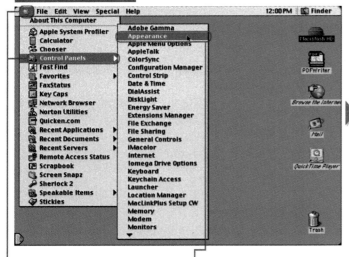

1 Click the Apple menu.

2 Choose **Control Panels**.

3 Choose **Appearance**.

4 Click the appropriate tabs
and make changes to your
current theme.

5 After you finish making
changes, click **Save Theme**
on the Themes tab.

Can I edit an existing theme?

Yes. Load the existing theme, make your changes, and then save the new theme with the same name as the original.

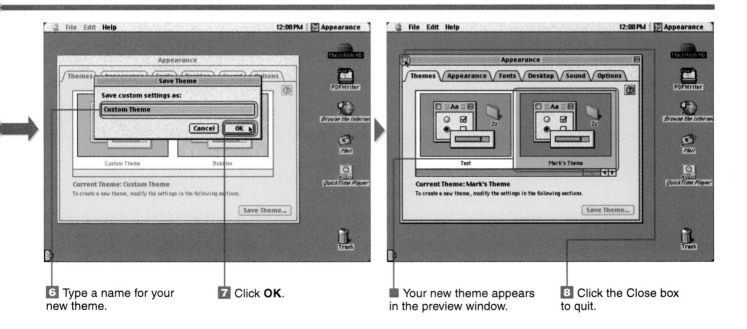

6 Type a name for your new theme.

7 Click **OK**.

■ Your new theme appears in the preview window.

8 Click the Close box to quit.

CLEAN UP AND SORT DESKTOP ICONS

You can neatly arrange icons on your desktop in sorted order.

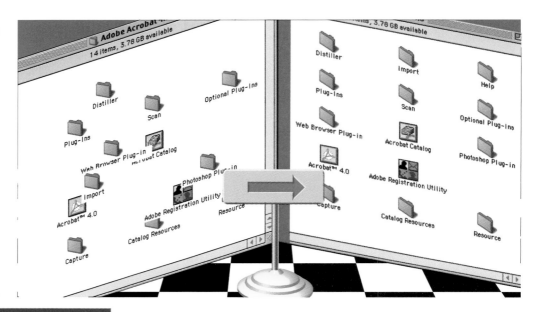

CLEAN UP AND SORT DESKTOP ICONS

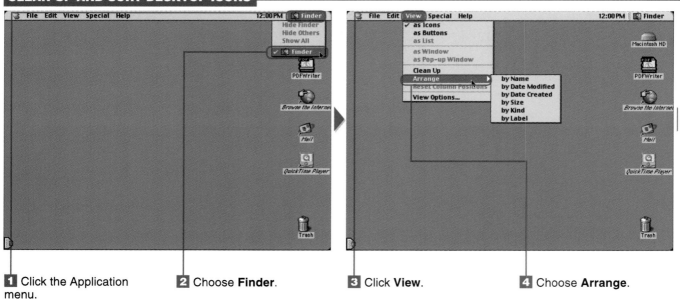

1 Click the Application menu.

2 Choose **Finder**.

3 Click **View**.

4 Choose **Arrange**.

I cannot use the Arrange menu item — what is wrong?

The Arrange menu item will not be available if you have selected the **Keep arranged** order in the View Options dialog box.

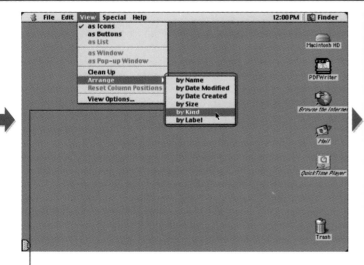

5 Select a sort criteria from the submenu.

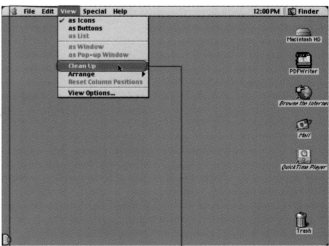

6 To straighten and realign icons on your desktop, click **View**.

7 Choose **Clean Up**.

MANUALLY ARRANGE DESKTOP ICONS

You can manually arrange your desktop icons.

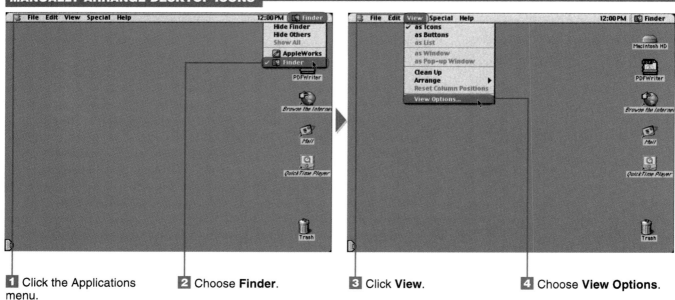

1 Click the Applications menu.

2 Choose **Finder**.

3 Click **View**.

4 Choose **View Options**.

**How do I return my desktop icons
back to their original location
after I have moved them?**

Click and drag the icons back to
their original positions, then click
View and choose **Clean Up** to
realign them.

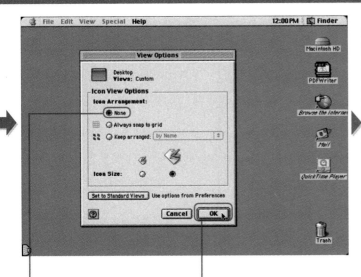

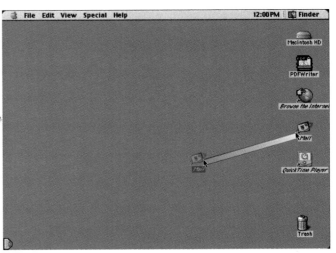

5 Click the **None** radio
button (○ changes to ◉).

6 Click **OK** to save your
changes.

7 Click and drag any
desktop icon to the desired
location, then release the
mouse button to drop it.

CHAPTER 6

Using a Printer

Eventually, you'll want to print out your documents. This chapter explains how to hook up and configure a printer.

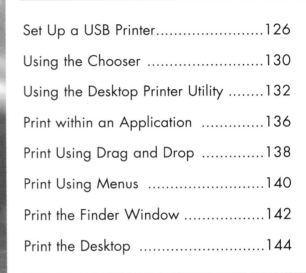

SET UP A USB PRINTER

Your printer should be turned off before you connect it to your iMac.

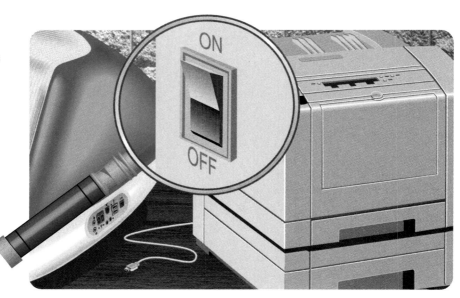

SET UP A USB PRINTER

1 Plug your USB printer into the AC wall socket, and make sure that it is turned off.

2 Load the USB drivers or printer software required by your printer.

I have an older Macintosh printer with a different cable connector. Can I use it with my iMac?

Yes, but you need a USB-to-serial converter to use an older Macintosh printer with the traditional printer connector. The iMac does not have a serial printer port. Before you purchase a converter, check the manufacturer's Web site to make sure your printer is compatible with the converter.

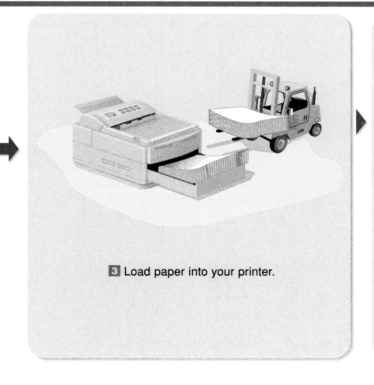

3 Load paper into your printer.

4 Turn on your printer.

CONTINUED

SET UP A USB PRINTER

You can connect your USB printer to your iMac without shutting down the iMac.

5 Restart your iMac.

6 Locate an open USB port on the right side of the case.

Will any USB printer work with my iMac?

No, not every printer supports the iMac! Without the proper drivers, a printer may not work with your iMac. So check the specifications for any printer you're considering to make sure that it's designed for your computer.

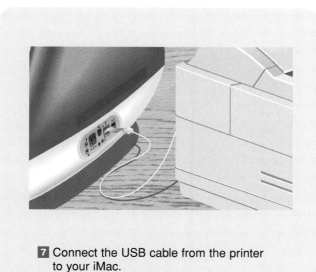

7 Connect the USB cable from the printer to your iMac.

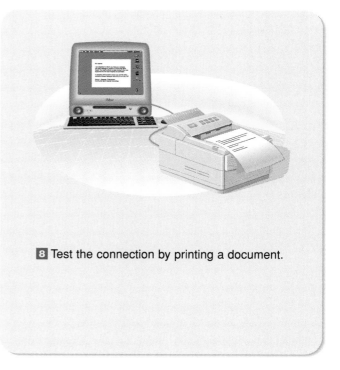

8 Test the connection by printing a document.

USING THE CHOOSER

You can use the Chooser
to set up a default
printer.

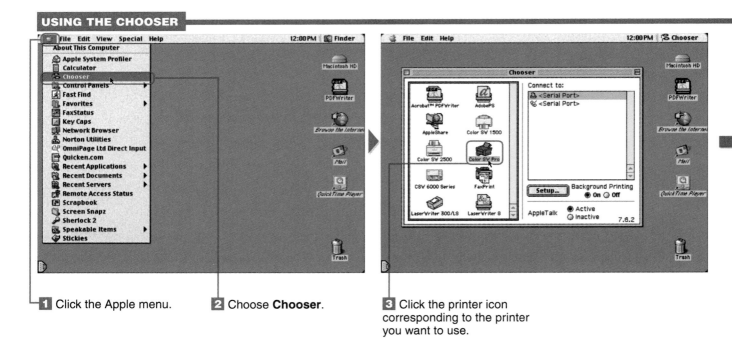

1 Click the Apple menu.

2 Choose **Chooser**.

3 Click the printer icon
corresponding to the printer
you want to use.

Can I use the Chooser while applications are running?

If you use the Chooser to select a new printer while other applications are running, you should display the Page Setup screen (and change values, if necessary) before printing from those open applications.

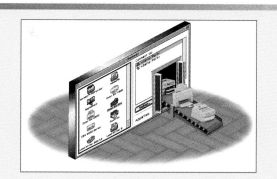

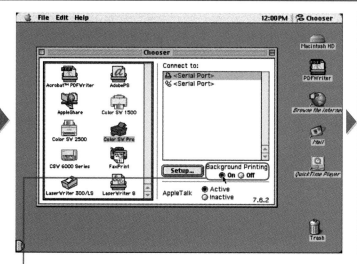

4 Set any configuration options specific to your printer.

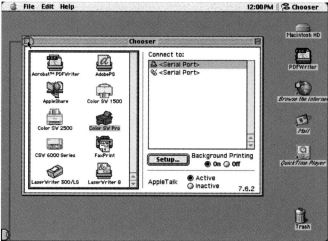

5 Click the Close box to save your selection.

USING THE DESKTOP PRINTER UTILITY

You may need to use the Desktop Printer Utility to set up some older Mac-compatible printers.

USING THE DESKTOP PRINTER UTILITY

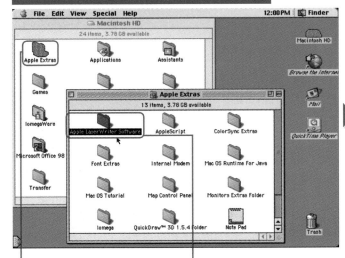

1 Open the Apple Extras folder.

2 Open the Apple LaserWriter Software folder.

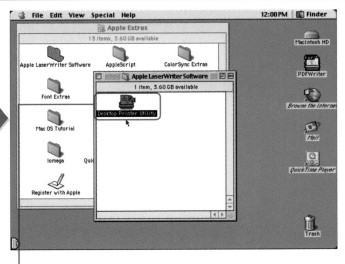

3 Double-click the Desktop Printer Utility.

I have more than one printer icon on my desktop. How can I select one as the default printer?

From the Finder, click the desired printer to highlight it, and click **Printing** and choose **Set Default Printer**.

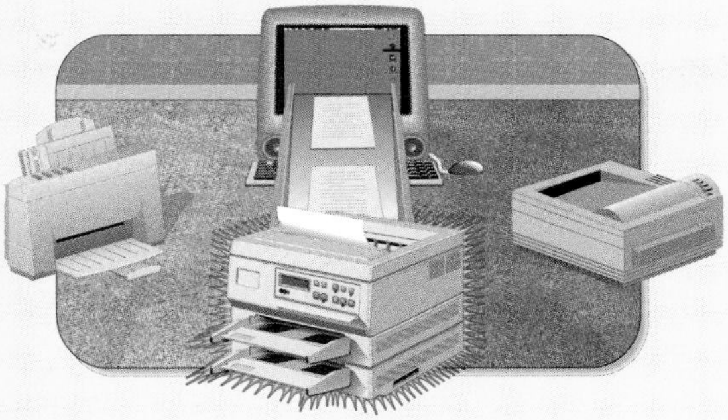

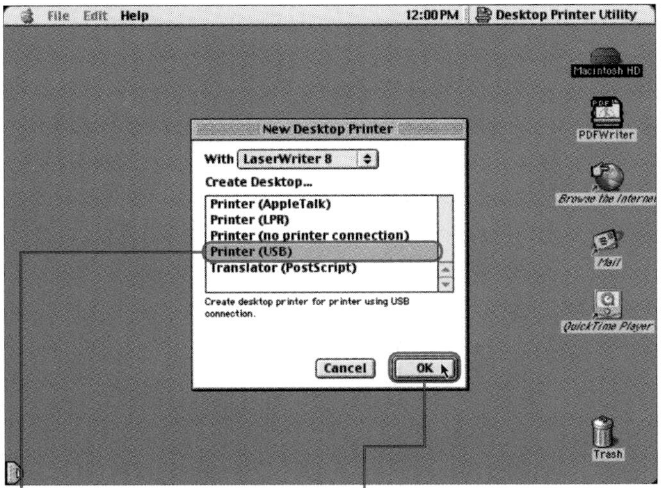

4 Choose the proper connection type for the printer you're adding to the desktop.

5 Click **OK** to continue.

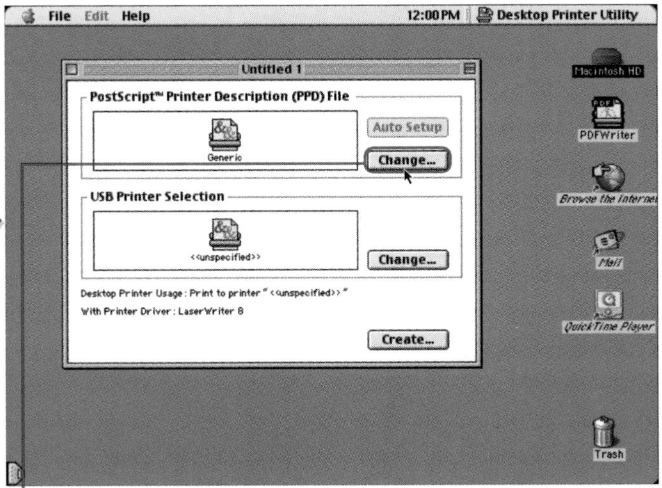

6 Click the **Change** button under PPD File.

CONTINUED

USING THE DESKTOP PRINTER UTILITY

The PPD file carries all
the printer configuration
information for the
printer you install.

USING THE DESKTOP PRINTER UTILITY

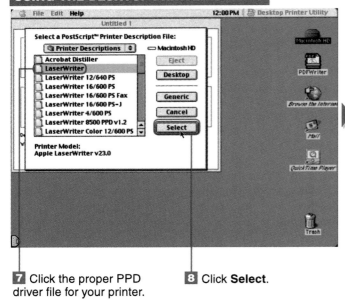

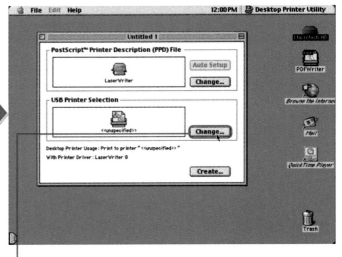

7 Click the proper PPD
driver file for your printer.

8 Click **Select**.

9 Click the **Change** button
under Printer Selection.

I don't see a PPD driver file for my printer! What should I do?

If you don't see a PPD specifically named after your printer, click **Generic** (which should work for most printers as an alternative PPD). Also, you may be able to set up your printer using the Chooser instead, as described in the previous section.

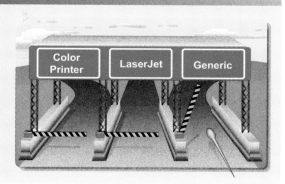

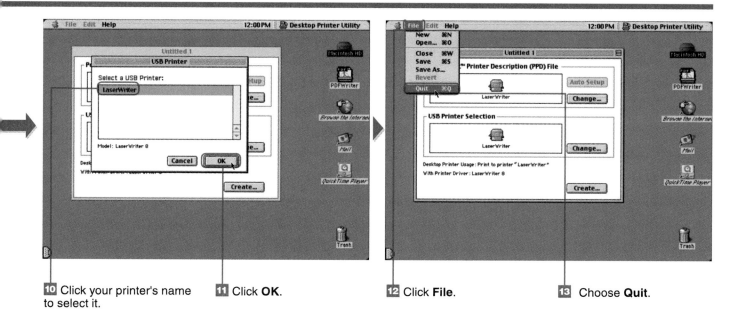

10 Click your printer's name to select it.

11 Click **OK**.

12 Click **File**.

13 Choose **Quit**.

PRINT WITHIN AN APPLICATION

Most of the documents
you print will probably
originate from within
an application that's
currently running on
your iMac.

PRINT WITHIN AN APPLICATION

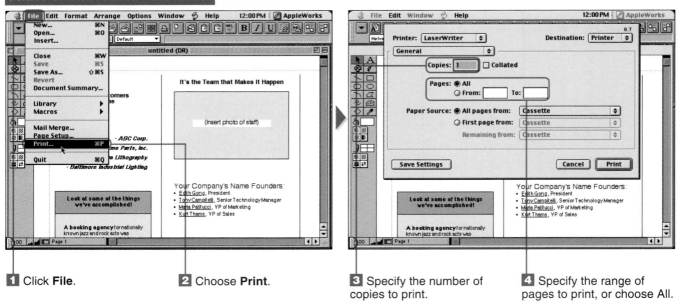

1 Click **File**.

2 Choose **Print**.

3 Specify the number of copies to print.

4 Specify the range of pages to print, or choose All.

What changes can I make to the advanced printer settings?

If advanced settings are available, they will vary according to the printer you're using — check your printer's user manual or display the online help for more information.

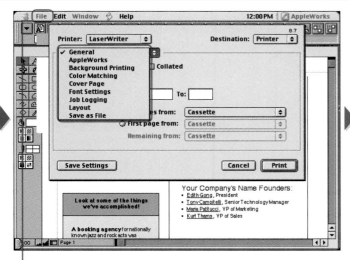

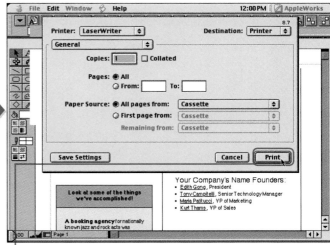

5 Click the Advanced or Options button or select the Settings drop-down list to display and change other printer settings.

6 Click **Print** to begin printing.

PRINT USING DRAG AND DROP

You can print a
document from the
desktop using the drag-
and-drop method.

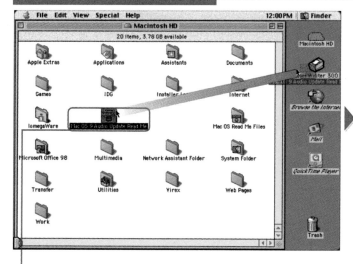

1 Click and drag the
document icon to the
desktop printer icon.

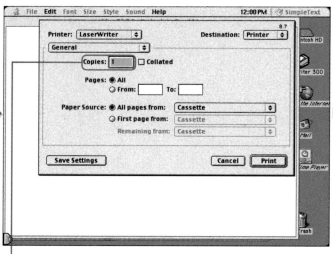

2 Specify the number of
copies to print.

Can I print multiple documents at once using drag and drop?

Yes. Just select all the documents you want to print and drag them to the desktop printer icon.

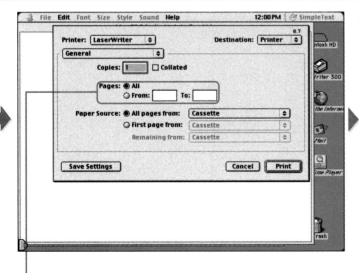

3 Specify the range of pages to print, or choose All.

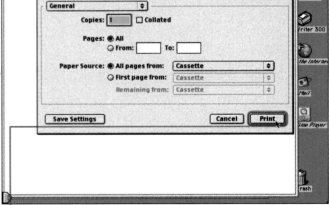

4 Click **Print** to send the document to your printer.

PRINT USING MENUS

You can also print a
document from the
desktop using the Finder
menu.

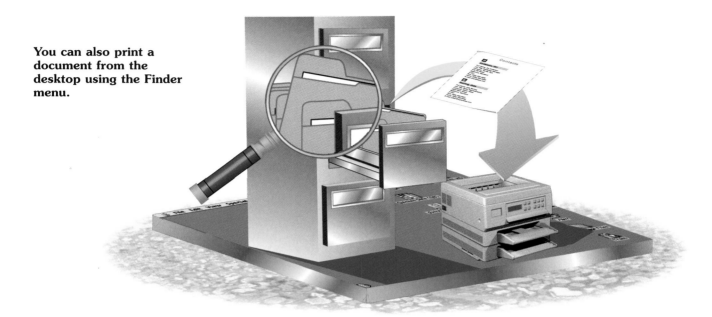

PRINT USING MENUS

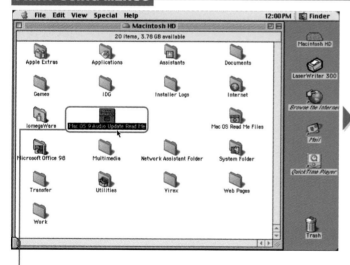

1 Click the document icon
to select it.

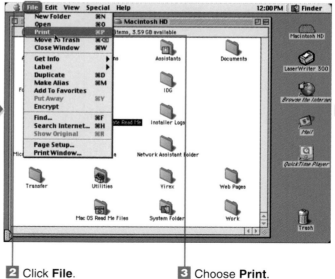

2 Click **File**.

3 Choose **Print**.

Why does the application launch when I print a document from the desktop?

Because the document is associated with a specific application, Mac OS 9 needs to open the application to print.

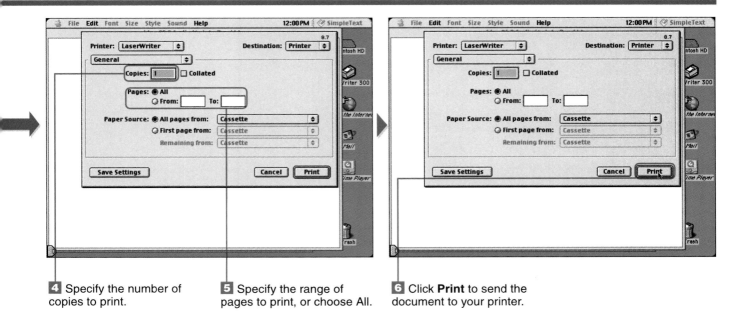

4 Specify the number of copies to print.

5 Specify the range of pages to print, or choose All.

6 Click **Print** to send the document to your printer.

PRINT THE FINDER WINDOW

You can print the
contents of the active
Finder window.

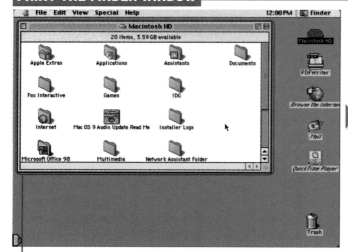

1 Click anywhere within the
borders of the window to
make it active.

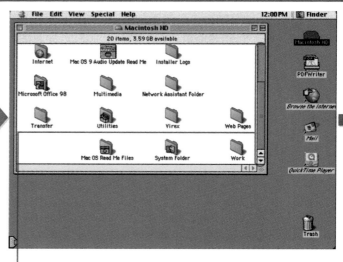

2 Scroll to display the
contents you want to print.

Why isn't the printed image in color?

You need a color printer to see a color printout of a window.

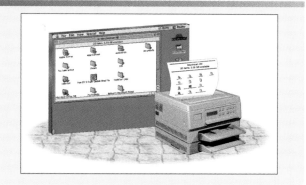

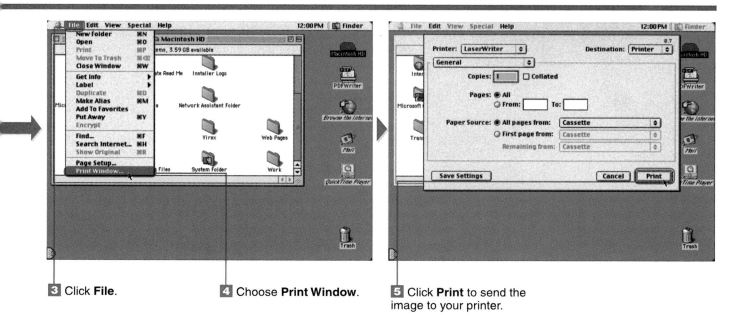

3 Click **File**.

4 Choose **Print Window**.

5 Click **Print** to send the image to your printer.

PRINT THE DESKTOP

You can print the
contents of your iMac's
desktop.

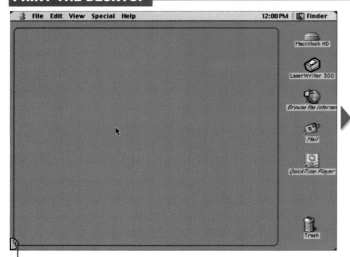

1 Click anywhere on the
desktop, but not on an icon.

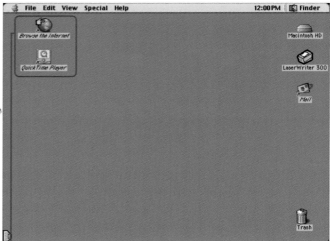

2 Arrange the icons and
windows on your desktop
as desired.

The printed image of my desktop is hard to read. How can I fix this?

Change the background for your desktop and increase the size of your View font to help make the contents easier to read.

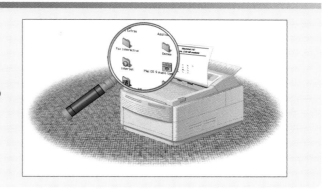

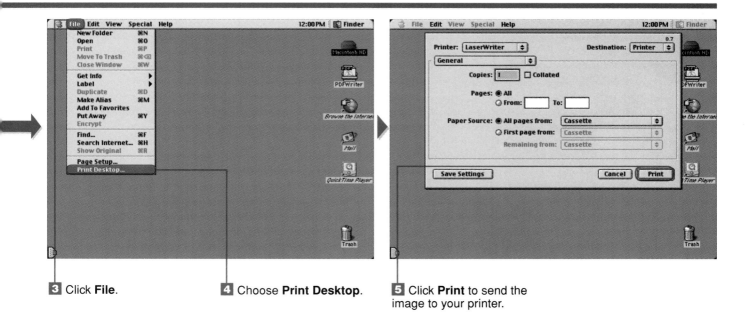

3 Click **File**.

4 Choose **Print Desktop**.

5 Click **Print** to send the image to your printer.

CHAPTER 7

Playing Audio, Video, and Speech

Did you know your iMac can talk to you? Indeed, it can. This chapter shows you how to configure speech on your iMac, as well as work with audio and video files.

SELECT AN ALERT SOUND

Your iMac uses an alert sound to attract your attention, and you can choose from a number of sounds that come with Mac OS 9.

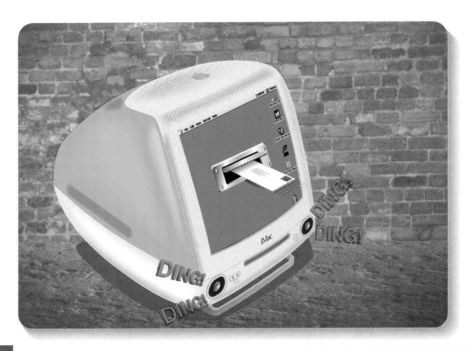

SELECT AN ALERT SOUND

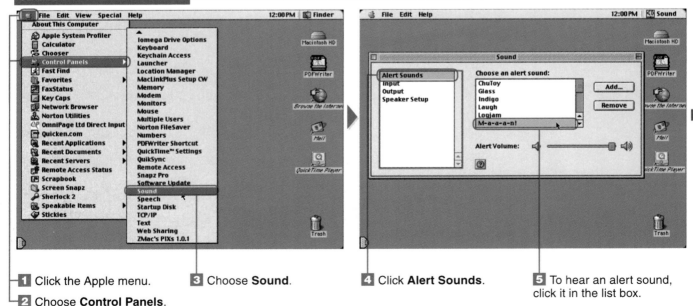

1 Click the Apple menu.

2 Choose **Control Panels**.

3 Choose **Sound**.

4 Click **Alert Sounds**.

5 To hear an alert sound, click it in the list box.

When will my iMac play an alert sound?

The alert sound is commonly played whenever a system event occurs, such as an error in a program or an important message from an application.

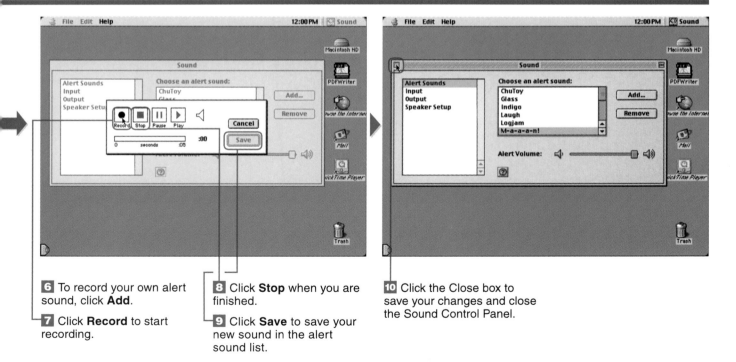

6 To record your own alert sound, click **Add**.

7 Click **Record** to start recording.

8 Click **Stop** when you are finished.

9 Click **Save** to save your new sound in the alert sound list.

10 Click the Close box to save your changes and close the Sound Control Panel.

SET AUDIO AND ALERT VOLUME

The Sound Control Panel enables you to select separate volume levels for the system alert sound and the audio output from your programs.

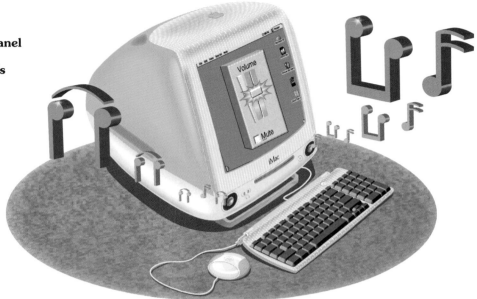

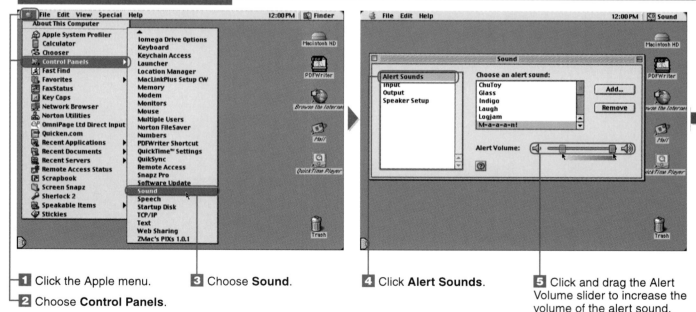

1 Click the Apple menu.

2 Choose **Control Panels**.

3 Choose **Sound**.

4 Click **Alert Sounds**.

5 Click and drag the Alert Volume slider to increase the volume of the alert sound.

How can I control the audio volume from the iMac desktop?

If you use the Control Strip, click the Speaker button and move the slider to set the volume.

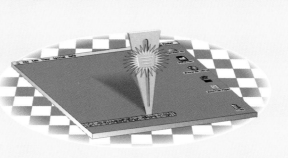

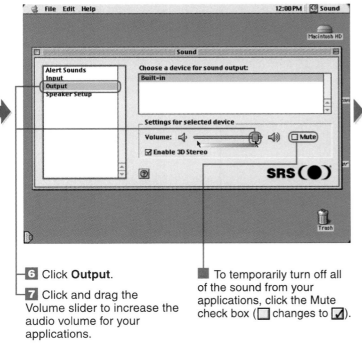

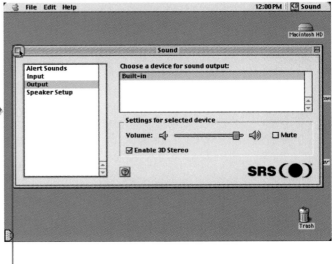

6 Click **Output**.

7 Click and drag the Volume slider to increase the audio volume for your applications.

■ To temporarily turn off all of the sound from your applications, click the Mute check box (☐ changes to ☑).

8 Click the Close box to save your changes and close the Sound Control Panel.

SET SPEAKER BALANCE

You can adjust the balance for your internal or external speakers from the Sound Control Panel.

SET SPEAKER BALANCE

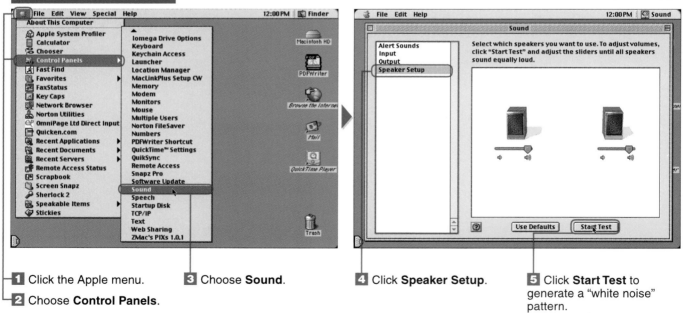

1 Click the Apple menu.

2 Choose **Control Panels**.

3 Choose **Sound**.

4 Click **Speaker Setup**.

5 Click **Start Test** to generate a "white noise" pattern.

Do I need to adjust the balance if I am using headphones?

No. The right and left sides of your headphones are already balanced.

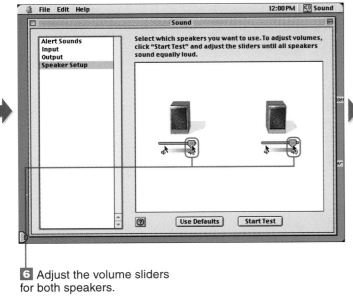

6 Adjust the volume sliders for both speakers.

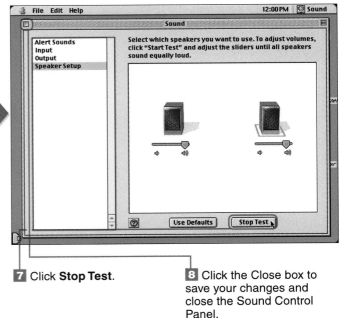

7 Click **Stop Test**.

8 Click the Close box to save your changes and close the Sound Control Panel.

USING 3-D SURROUND SOUND

Your iMac can produce 3-D SRS stereo effects while playing audio CDs, DVDs, or games. The 3-D effect works best with external speakers.

USING 3-D SURROUND SOUND

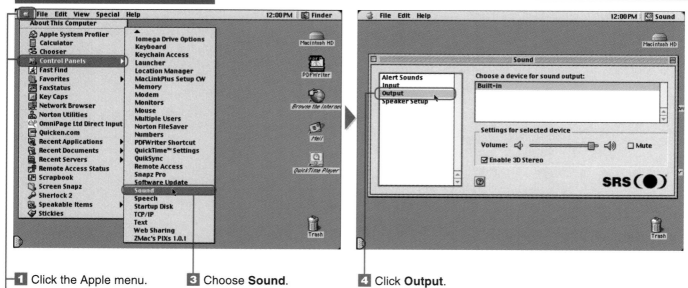

1 Click the Apple menu.

2 Choose **Control Panels**.

3 Choose **Sound**.

4 Click **Output**.

154

Does a game have to specifically support 3-D SRS sound?

No. Even games that do not directly support SRS still make limited use of 3-D positional sound if you enable the 3-D stereo function.

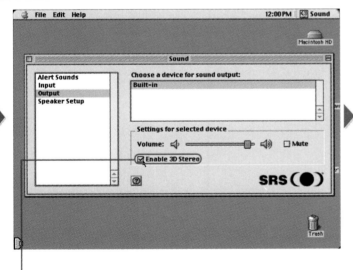

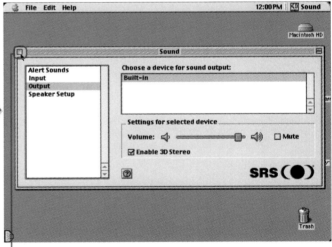

5 Click the Enable 3D Stereo check box to enable it (☐ changes to ☑).

6 Click the Close box to save your changes and close the Sound Control Panel.

WATCH A QUICKTIME MOVIE

Apple's QuickTime
Player can play a variety
of multimedia files,
including movies.

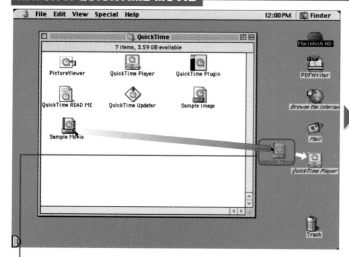

1 Drag the movie's icon to the QuickTime Player icon.

2 Click the Play button to run the movie.

3 Click the Pause button to stop the movie and display a still image.

What formats does QuickTime Player support?

It can display video in AVI, MPEG, and MOOV formats, as well as JPEG pictures. QuickTime Player can also play AIFF digital audio.

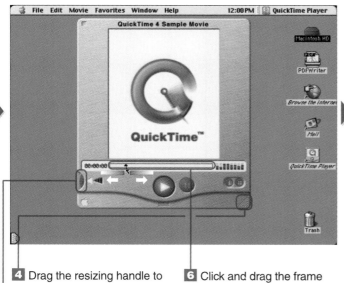

4 Drag the resizing handle to enlarge or shrink the display.

5 Click and drag the rotary volume control to adjust the volume.

6 Click and drag the frame slider to rewind or fast-forward.

7 Click the Close box to close the movie.

SELECT A VOICE

With the Speech feature, you can hear from your computer in a wide range of voices!

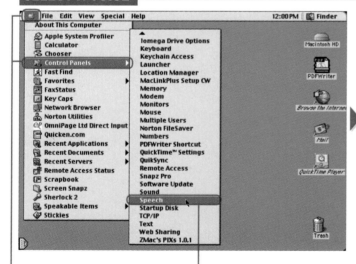

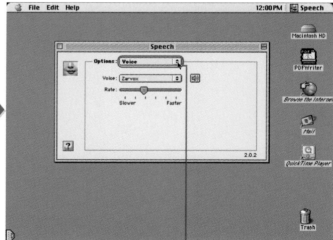

1 Click the Apple menu.

2 Choose **Control Panels**.

3 Choose **Speech**.

■ The Speech Control Panel appears.

4 Click the Options drop-down list box and select **Voice**.

Can my iMac read a text file?

Yes. Open the text file using
SimpleText, choose **Sound**, and
choose **Speak All**. You can also
select a part of the text by
highlighting it; your iMac speaks
only that text.

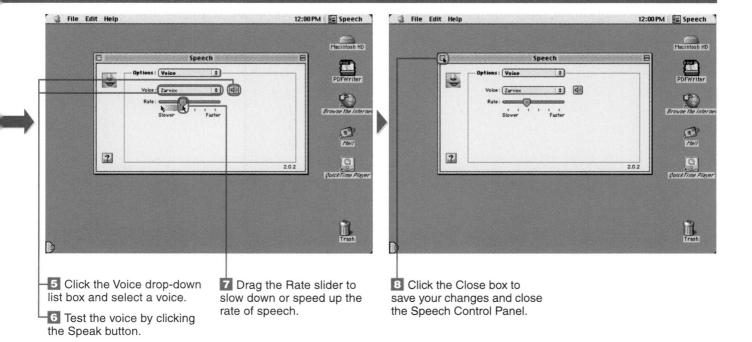

5 Click the Voice drop-down
list box and select a voice.

6 Test the voice by clicking
the Speak button.

7 Drag the Rate slider to
slow down or speed up the
rate of speech.

8 Click the Close box to
save your changes and close
the Speech Control Panel.

USING TALKING ALERTS

You can program your iMac to speak an alert phrase after your alert sound. It can also read error messages to you.

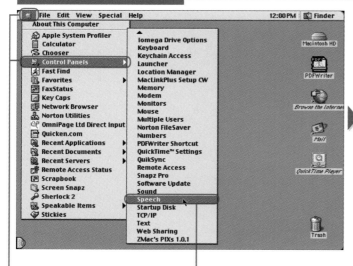

1 Click the Apple menu.

2 Choose **Control Panels**.

3 Choose **Speech**.

■ The Speech Control Panel appears.

4 Click the Options drop-down list box and select **Voice**.

Does Talking Alerts work with all my applications?

Yes. However, some applications generate alert and error messages that cannot be pronounced easily, and your iMac may not be able to read them correctly.

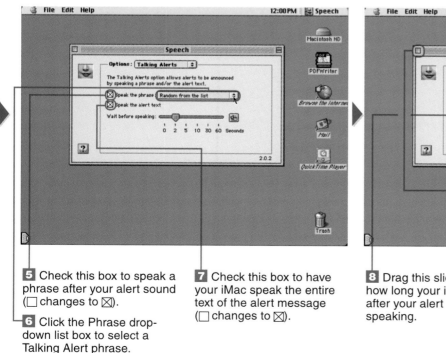

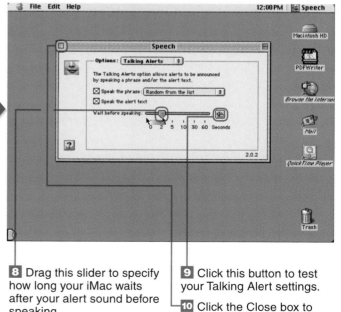

5 Check this box to speak a phrase after your alert sound (☐ changes to ☒).

6 Click the Phrase drop-down list box to select a Talking Alert phrase.

7 Check this box to have your iMac speak the entire text of the alert message (☐ changes to ☒).

8 Drag this slider to specify how long your iMac waits after your alert sound before speaking.

9 Click this button to test your Talking Alert settings.

10 Click the Close box to save your changes and close the Speech Control Panel.

USING SPEAKABLE ITEMS

With Speakable Items, you can control your iMac with your voice. For example, you can make menu choices within an application by speaking the menu name.

SHUT ➤
DOWN ➤

USING SPEAKABLE ITEMS

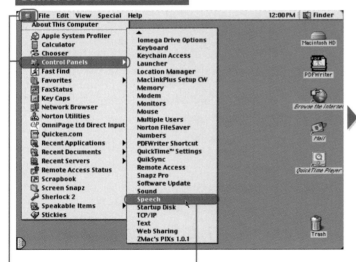

1 Click the Apple menu.

2 Choose **Control Panels**.

3 Choose **Speech**.

■ The Speech Control Panel appears.

4 Click the Options list box and choose **Speakable Items**.

How can I run applications and open documents?

Create an alias for a file or application in your Speakable Items folder. Your iMac recognizes the names of files in this special folder, so that you can run them by speaking their names. The Speakable Items folder is in your Apple Menu Items folder within your System Folder.

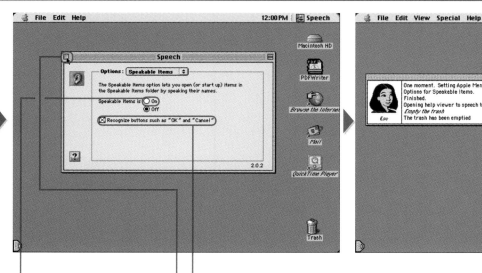

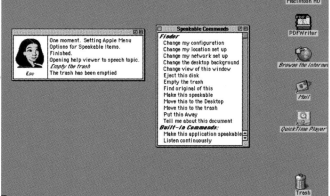

5 Click this radio button to turn on Speakable Items (O changes to ◉).

6 If you want to control dialog box buttons with your voice, click this check box (☐ changes to ☒).

7 Click the Close box to save your changes.

8 Press your Listening Key (Esc by default) whenever you want to speak a command.

CAPTURE VIDEO CLIPS WITH IMOVIE

If you are using an iMac equipped with a FireWire port, you can use iMovie to capture digital video footage by connecting a digital camera or DV (Digital Video) camera with a FireWire IEEE 1394 connector.

CAPTURE VIDEO CLIPS WITH **IMOVIE**

1 Click the Camera Mode button.

2 Click the Play button to begin the playback in the monitor.

How can I add a still image to my iMovie project?

If the still image is currently stored on your iMac, you can import it by clicking **File** and choosing **Import File**. This places the image as a ten-second still clip on your Clip Shelf.

3 When you are ready to start capturing video, click **Import**.

■ You can also press the Space bar to record.

4 To stop capturing, click **Import** again.

■ iMovie adds your new video clip to the Clip Shelf, where you can use it in your video projects.

EDIT VIDEO CLIPS WITH IMOVIE

After you capture the digital video you need for your video project, you can use iMovie to edit the individual clips into a movie.

EDIT VIDEO CLIPS WITH IMOVIE

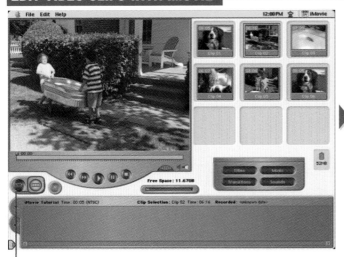

1 Click the Edit Mode button.

2 To add a clip to your film, drag it from the Clip Shelf to the Movie Track in the Clip Viewer.

■ To select multiple clips, hold down the Shift key.

How do I remove a clip from my movie?

To remove a clip, drag it from the Movie Track to your Clip Shelf.

3 To rearrange the order of clips, drag the clip to the desired position in the Clip Viewer.

4 To preview your movie while you are editing, click Play Movie Full Screen.

ADD TRANSITIONS

Transitions are ways to move from clip to clip in your movie. They add a professional touch to your iMovie projects.

1 Click **Transitions**.

2 Select a transition from the Transition Palette.

**Can I preview a transition before I
save my project?**

Yes. Click the transition's icon in
the Clip Viewer to select it and
click **Play**.

3 Drag the Duration slider
to change the speed of the
transition.

4 When finished, drag the
transition from the Transition
Palette to where you want it
in the Clip Viewer.

CHAPTER 8

Connecting to the Internet

The iMac was made with the Internet in mind. In this chapter, you discover how to connect to an Internet service provider.

FISHING GUIDE

When was the last time you heard someone boast about the trophy largemouth bass they reeled in on their last fishing outing? Have you always wanted to go fishing but didn't know where to start? Whether you assume this popular sport is as easy as finding a pond and plopping yourself down with a line, or whether you are intimidated by the large array of rods, reels, baits, lures and fish, these few basic guidelines will help you get started. The choices in the world of fishing are enormous. Do you want to fish for fun, for trophy or for supper? Are you looking for a particular type of fish or for the most convenient location? Are you handy with a boat or more comfortable sticking to shore?

No matter what your preferences are, try to choose a quiet location in the cool still of the early morning or evening. Make sure you are aware of the weather forecast before you set out so you can dress appropriately. Remember that temperatures are often cooler by the water, with different wind factors. Don't be discouraged by light rain since some of the best fishing can be done in the rain! And don't forget to pack plenty to eat for an enjoyable outing.

Some good guides to fishing spots in your area can be obtained from local tourism information.

How does the Internet work? Of course, an in-depth technical explanation of the Internet is beyond the scope of this book, but this chapter gives you an overview of its basic structure and function.

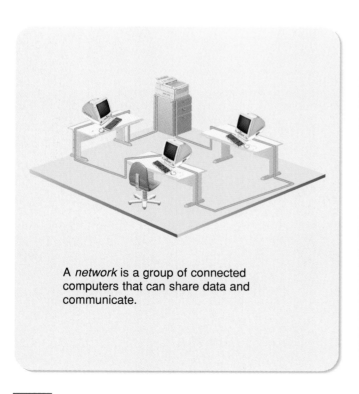

A *network* is a group of connected computers that can share data and communicate.

When a computer is connected to the Internet, it can talk to any other computer around the world!

Most home computers connect to the Internet through an **Internet service provider** (ISP). An ISP usually offers you an e-mail address and Web page, too.

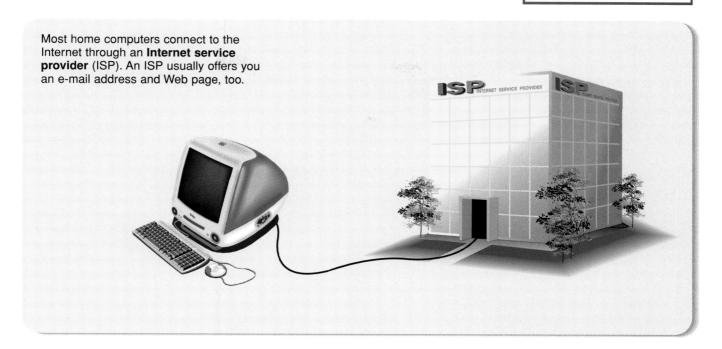

Each computer on the Internet is identified by a unique number called an *IP address.* Think of your IP address as your Internet mailing address.

Your ISP automatically provides your iMac with an IP address when you connect.

CONNECT TO AN EXISTING ISP

If you already have an account with an Internet service provider, follow the steps in this section.

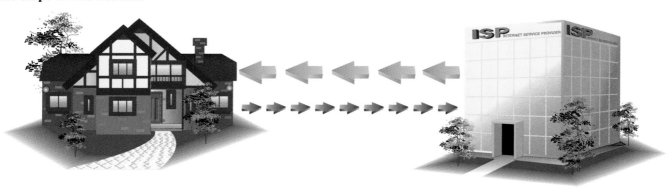

CONNECT TO AN EXISTING ISP

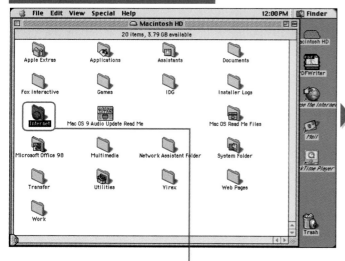

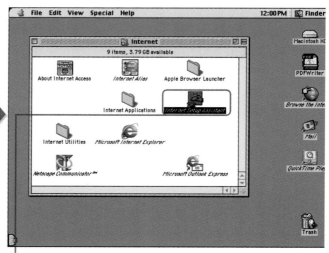

1 Open your hard drive.

2 Open the Internet folder.

3 Double-click the Internet Setup Assistant.

How can I correct a mistake while using the Internet Setup Assistant?

If you need to back up one or more steps to correct a mistake, click the arrow pointing to the left.

4 Click **Yes** to continue.

5 Click **Yes** to indicate that you want to set up an existing account.

CONTINUED

CONNECT TO AN EXISTING ISP

If you don't have your
existing Internet account
configuration written
down, ask your ISP to
provide you with this
information.

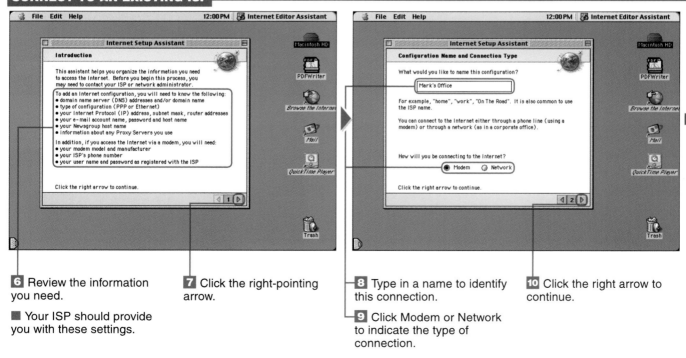

6 Review the information
you need.

■ Your ISP should provide
you with these settings.

7 Click the right-pointing
arrow.

8 Type in a name to identify
this connection.

9 Click Modem or Network
to indicate the type of
connection.

10 Click the right arrow to
continue.

**I'm using a network connection.
Do these steps still apply to me?**

If you're using a network
connection, you can still follow
along — just skip Steps 11
through 19.

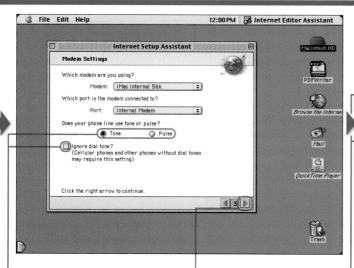

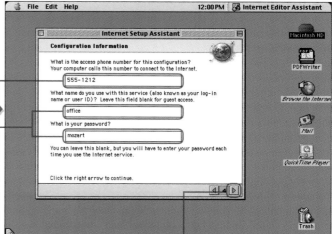

11 If you're using a modem,
click Tone or Pulse to select
the dialing method (usually
Tone).

12 If you're using a cellular
or PDX system with no dial
tone, click the Ignore Dial
Tone check box.

13 Click the right arrow to
continue.

14 Enter the phone number
your iMac should call.

15 Type in your account
username and the
password.

16 Click on the right arrow to
continue.

CONTINUED

CONNECT TO AN EXISTING ISP

You can usually accept the defaults provided by the Internet Setup Assistant. The defaults apply to the majority of iMac owners.

CONNECT TO AN EXISTING ISP

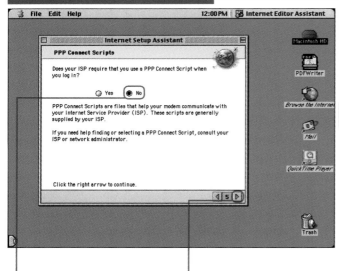

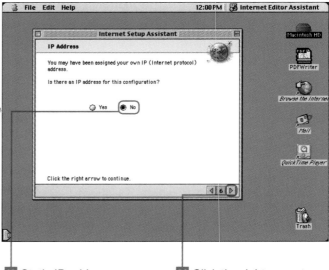

17 Almost all ISPs do not require a PPP script, so click No.

18 Click the right arrow to continue.

19 Static IP addresses are rarely used, so click No.

20 Click the right arrow to continue.

My e-mail address doesn't end in .com. Is something wrong with it?

Most e-mail addresses are in the form `yourname@yourisp.com`, but others may end in `.net`, `.org`, or another extension. This is a naming convention and doesn't affect your connection.

ORGANIZATION

com	commercial
edu	education
gov	government
mil	military
net	network
org	organization (often non-profit)

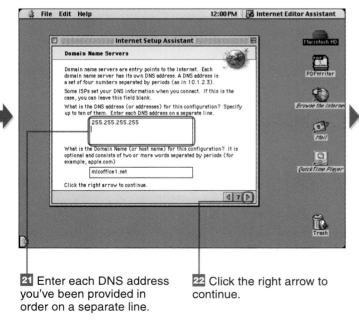

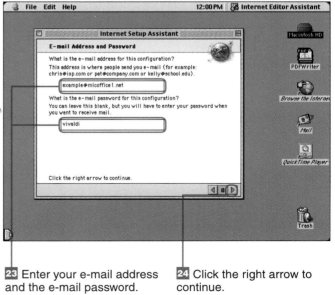

21 Enter each DNS address you've been provided in order on a separate line.

22 Click the right arrow to continue.

23 Enter your e-mail address and the e-mail password.

24 Click the right arrow to continue.

CONTINUED

CONNECT TO AN EXISTING ISP

Your ISP may include access to an Internet newsgroup service along with your e-mail service.

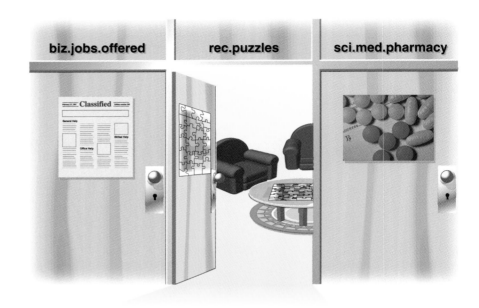

CONNECT TO AN EXISTING ISP

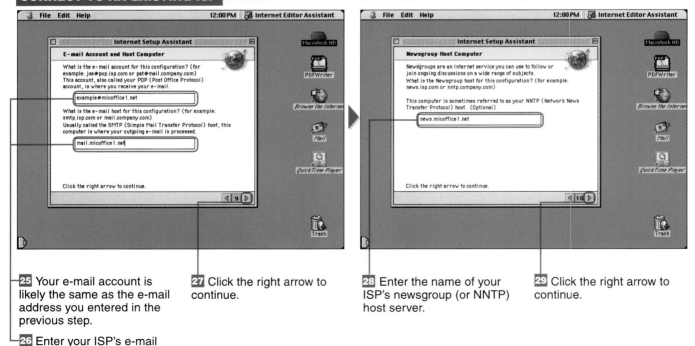

25 Your e-mail account is likely the same as the e-mail address you entered in the previous step.

26 Enter your ISP's e-mail host name.

27 Click the right arrow to continue.

28 Enter the name of your ISP's newsgroup (or NNTP) host server.

29 Click the right arrow to continue.

**I don't want my iMac to
automatically log on to the
Internet. How can I fix this?**

For greater security, you can leave
the password fields blank to
prevent an automatic logon; your
iMac prompts you for your
password each time you connect.

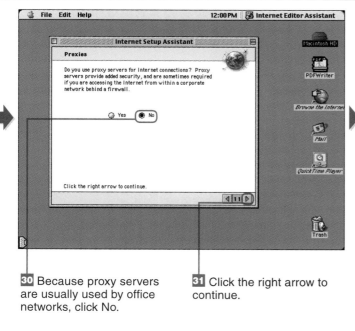

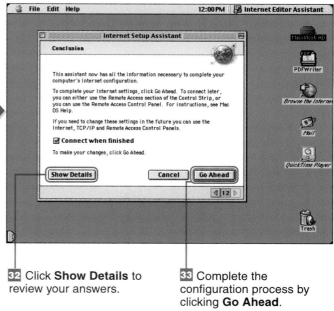

30 Because proxy servers
are usually used by office
networks, click No.

31 Click the right arrow to
continue.

32 Click **Show Details** to
review your answers.

33 Complete the
configuration process by
clicking **Go Ahead**.

SELECT AND CONNECT WITH A NEW ISP

If you haven't selected
an Internet service
provider yet, the Internet
Setup Assistant can help
you subscribe and get
online.

SELECT AND CONNECT WITH A NEW ISP

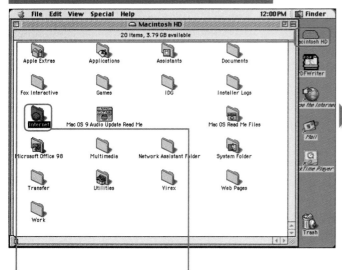

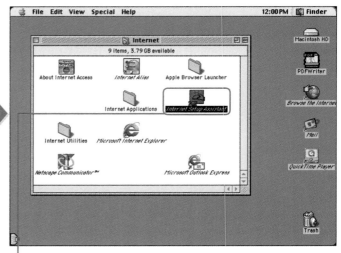

1 Open your hard drive.

2 Open the Internet folder.

3 Double-click the Internet
Setup Assistant.

**Does my modem have to be
connected to sign up with an ISP?**

Yes. Your iMac must dial in and
connect with the referral system,
so it does need to be connected to
the wall telephone jack.

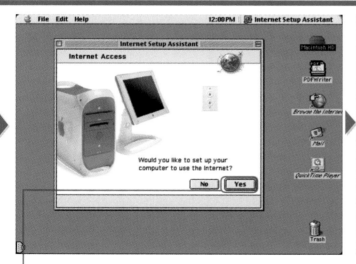

4 Click **Yes** to continue.

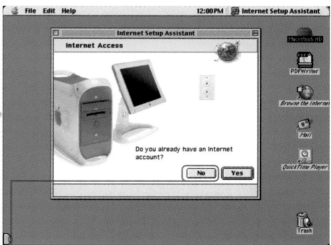

5 Click **No** to indicate that
you do not have an existing
ISP account.

CONTINUED

SELECT AND CONNECT WITH A NEW ISP

The Internet Setup Assistant searches for a local ISP based on your area code and telephone number.

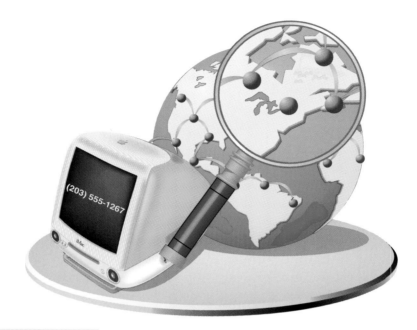

SELECT AND CONNECT WITH A NEW ISP

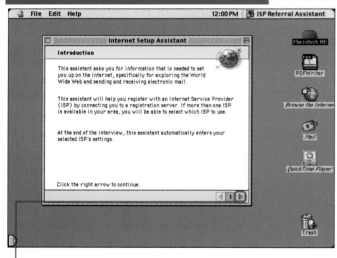

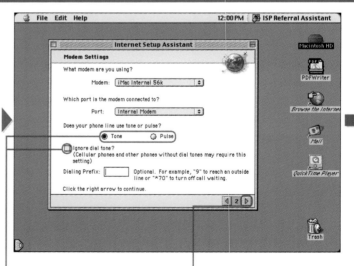

6 Click the right arrow to continue.

7 Click Tone or Pulse to select the dialing method (usually Tone).

8 If you're using a cellular or PDX system with no dial tone, click the Ignore Dial Tone check box.

9 Click the right arrow to continue.

**Is it a good idea to connect to an
ISP located out of town?**

As long as the number is in your
local calling area. Avoid calling
any ISP long distance unless
absolutely necessary, because you
quickly incur a huge telephone bill!

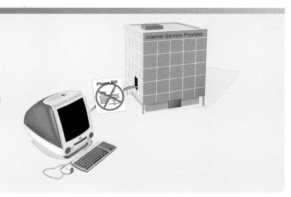

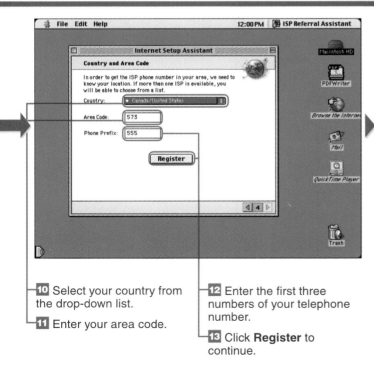

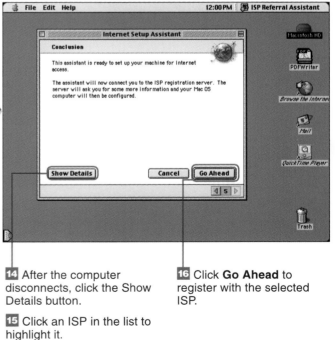

10 Select your country from
the drop-down list.

11 Enter your area code.

12 Enter the first three
numbers of your telephone
number.

13 Click **Register** to
continue.

14 After the computer
disconnects, click the Show
Details button.

15 Click an ISP in the list to
highlight it.

16 Click **Go Ahead** to
register with the selected
ISP.

CHAPTER 9

Browsing the Web

Your iMac comes with Microsoft Internet Explorer, and this chapter explores how to use it to surf the Web.

LAUNCH AND QUIT INTERNET EXPLORER

You can use Internet
Explorer to browse the
Web.

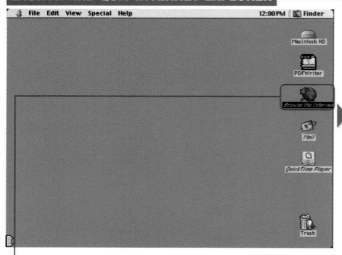

LAUNCH AND QUIT INTERNET EXPLORER

1 Click the Browse the
Internet icon on your
desktop to launch your
browser.

■ If you do not have a
Browse the Internet icon on
your desktop, navigate to
the Internet Explorer
application on your hard
drive.

2 To quit, click **File**.

3 Choose **Quit**.

THE INTERNET EXPLORER INTERFACE

Here are the essential parts of the Internet Explorer interface.

Back and Forward Buttons

Use the buttons to navigate between pages.

Address Bar

Shows the Web address.

Browser Window

Displays the content of the Web page.

Link

An underlined word or phrase that, when clicked, takes you to another Web page. Pictures can also be links.

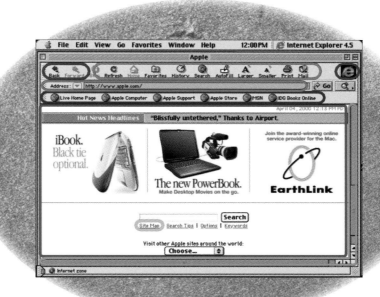

Activity Icon

Moves when your browser loads a Web page.

Button Bar

Displays common browser commands.

Favorites Bar

Can hold your most frequently visited sites.

Scroll Bars

Used to display information that doesn't fit inside the browser window.

ENTER A WEB ADDRESS MANUALLY

Often, you need to enter a *Web address* for a Web site manually — for example, from a book or magazine.

URL

http://www.flowerstop.com

ENTER A WEB ADDRESS MANUALLY

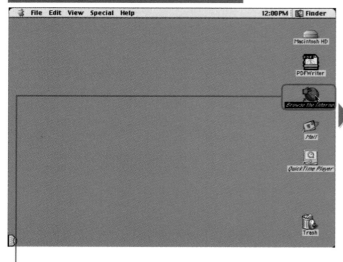

1 Click the Browse the Internet icon.

2 Highlight all the text in the Address field.

Is there a keyboard shortcut to replace the Go button?

Yes. Press the Return key to load the page after you type the full address.

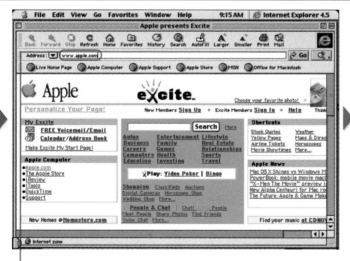

3 Enter the text exactly as printed without the **http**:// part.

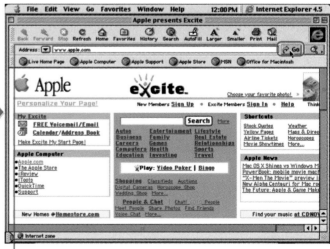

4 Click the **Go** button.

ENTER A WEB ADDRESS USING CUT AND PASTE

If you want to enter a
Web address from an
open document in
another application, use
the cut-and-paste
method.

ENTER A WEB ADDRESS USING CUT AND PASTE

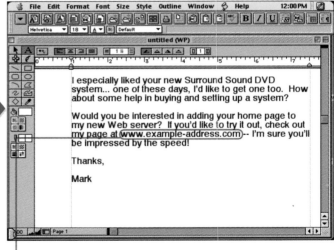

1 If necessary, click the
application window to make
it active.

2 Display the address you
want to copy.

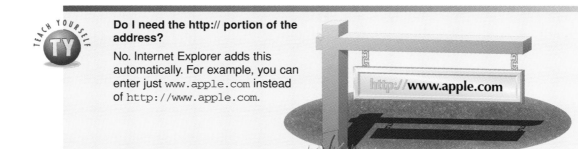

Do I need the http:// portion of the address?

No. Internet Explorer adds this automatically. For example, you can enter just www.apple.com instead of http://www.apple.com.

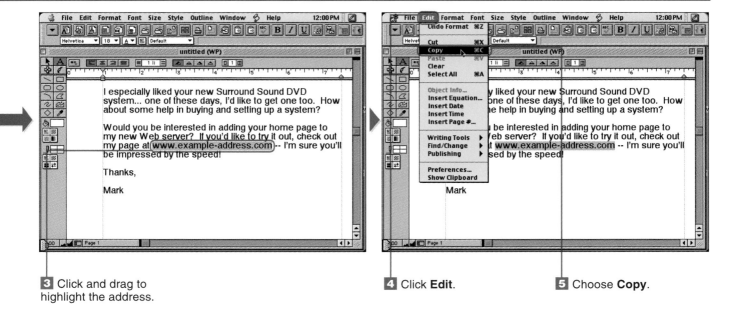

3 Click and drag to highlight the address.

4 Click **Edit**.

5 Choose **Copy**.

CONTINUED

ENTER A WEB ADDRESS USING CUT AND PASTE

After you copy the address to the Clipboard, you can paste it into Internet Explorer.

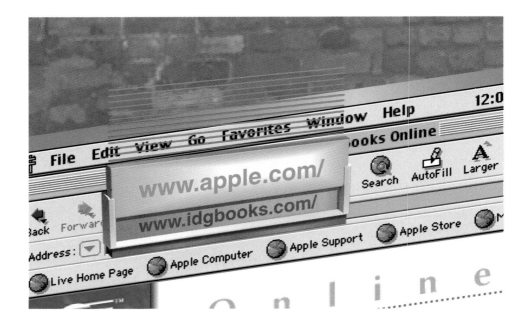

ENTER A WEB ADDRESS USING CUT AND PASTE

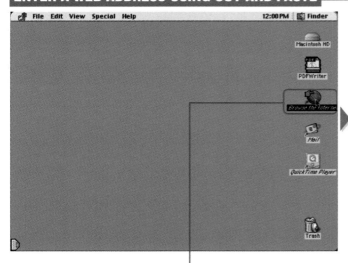

6 Return to the desktop.

7 Click the Browse the Internet icon.

8 Highlight all the text in the Address field.

Do I have to cut and paste a Web address if it's underlined in the document?

Not always. The underline may indicate that the Web address is a *link* (just like the links on a Web page). Try clicking on the address in the document. If it's a link, Internet Explorer automatically loads and takes you to that site.

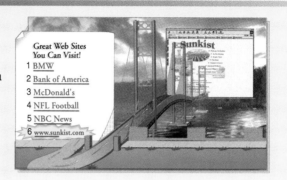

Great Web Sites
You Can Visit!
1 BMW
2 Bank of America
3 McDonald's
4 NFL Football
5 NBC News
6 www.sunkist.com

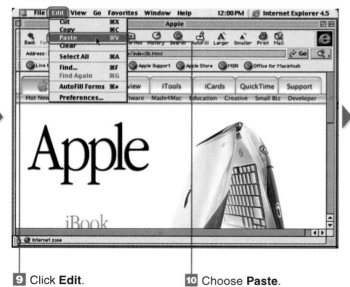

9 Click **Edit**.

10 Choose **Paste**.

11 Click the Go button (or press Return).

ENTER PARTIAL WEB ADDRESSES

Internet Explorer has a feature called *AutoComplete*, which enables you to enter partial addresses in the Address field; IE may be able to complete the address for you, if you've visited the site before.

ENTER PARTIAL WEB ADDRESSES

1 Highlight all the text in the Address field.

2 Type a key word of the address.

Will AutoComplete work with sites that I haven't visited?

No. AutoComplete isn't a replacement for a Web search engine like Sherlock 2. It searches only the URLs that you've already visited.

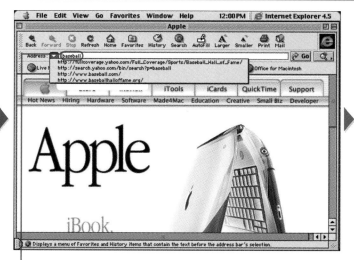

3 Click the down arrow next to the address field.

4 Click the address that you'd like to go to.

MOVE FORWARD AND BACKWARD

Click Back to return through the pages you've already seen in reverse order. After using the Back button, click Forward to advance through the pages to your original location.

MOVE FORWARD AND BACKWARD

1 Click **Back** to return to the previous page.

2 Click **Back** and hold the mouse button down to see a list of sites you've visited.

**The Back and Forward buttons
are grayed out and disabled.
Why?**

You must jump at least two pages
using text or graphic links before
the Back button is enabled. If you
click **Back** at least once, the
Forward button is enabled.

BACK HOME PAGE FORWARD

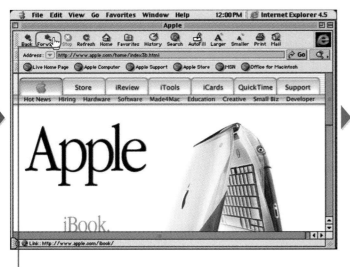

3 Click **Forward** to
advance a single page.

4 If you clicked the Back
button, click **Forward** and
hold the mouse button down
to see the list of sites you
cycled back through.

REFRESH AND STOP A WEB PAGE

From time-to-time, you may need to *refresh* (or reload) a Web page. You can also use the Stop button to stop the loading of a Web page.

1 Load the page in Internet Explorer.

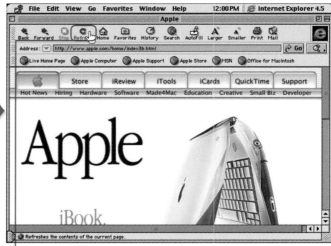

2 Click **Refresh** to reload the current Web page.

My browser doesn't have a Refresh button!

If you're using Netscape Navigator as your Web browser instead of Internet Explorer, the Refresh function is known as the Reload function.

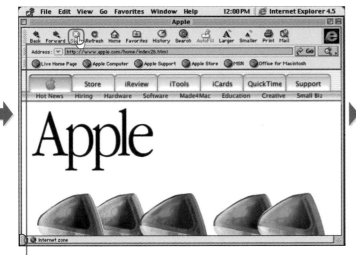

3 Click **Stop** to stop the loading of the current page.

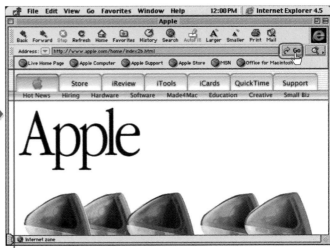

4 To restart the loading of the current page, click **Go**.

SET A HOME PAGE

By setting a home page within Internet Explorer, you can load and display a specific Web page each time you launch Internet Explorer. You can also return to your home page at any time with a click of a button.

SET A HOME PAGE

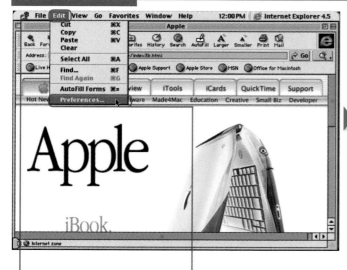

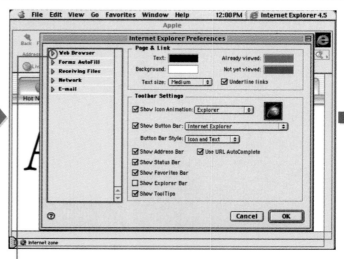

1 Click **Edit**.

2 Choose **Preferences**.

3 Click the triangle next to Web Browser to expand the category.

A home page takes too long to load. Can I just start with a blank page?

Yes. Instead of entering an address, click **Use None**.

Home, Blank Home

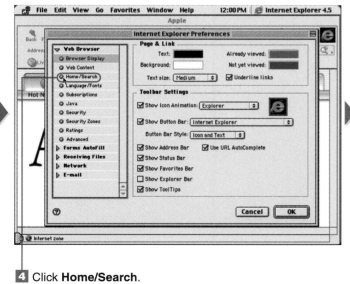

4 Click **Home/Search**.

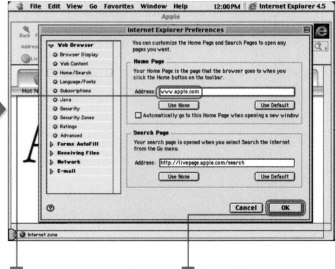

5 Type the address of the site you want to use in the Home Page Address field.

6 Click **OK** to save your changes.

JUMP TO A NEW WEB PAGE

A *link* is a line of text or an image on a Web page that automatically takes you to another location on the Web when you click it.

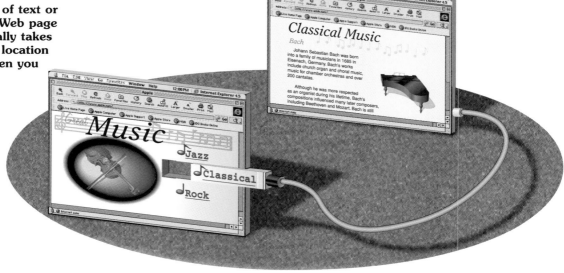

1 Click an underlined text link to jump.

2 Click a picture link to jump.

How can I tell which elements of a Web page are links?

Move your cursor over it; your cursor turns into a pointing finger to indicate a link. To use the link, click when the pointing finger appears.

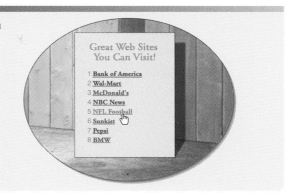

3 Click a button or icon to jump.

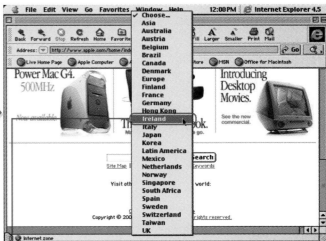

4 Click a drop-down list and select an entry to jump.

USING THE FAVORITES BAR

Internet Explorer can store the sites you visit often in a special category called *favorites*. You can add a favorite to the Favorite bar

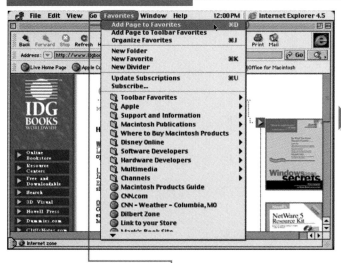

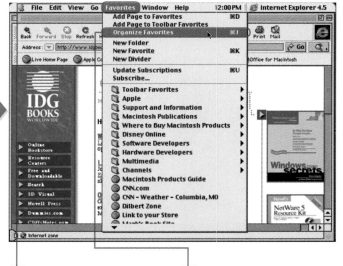

1 Load the Web page that you want to save as a favorite.

2 Click **Favorites**.

3 Choose **Add Page to Favorites**.

4 Click **Favorites**.

5 Choose **Organize Favorites**.

**I'm using Netscape Navigator, and
I don't see Favorites anywhere!**

Netscape Navigator users call
Favorites by another name:
Bookmarks.

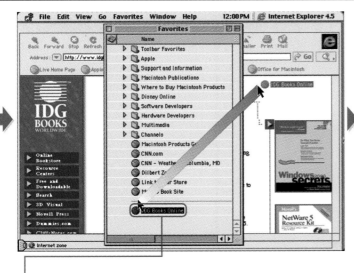

6 Drag the page icon to the
Toolbar Favorites folder.

7 Click the new favorite on
the Favorite bar to load the
site.

USING THE HISTORY FEATURE

Internet Explorer automatically maintains a History list of sites that you visit, and you can use the History list to return to pages that you didn't add to your Favorites list.

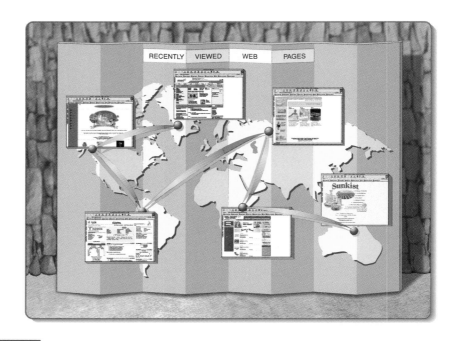

USING THE HISTORY FEATURE

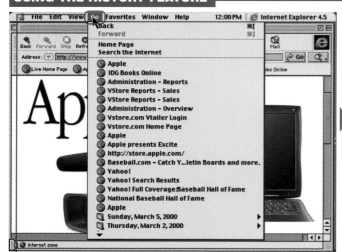

1 Click Go to show the pages that you visited during the current session.

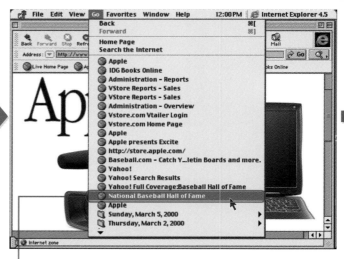

2 To return to a page, click the name.

Can I use entries from the History list elsewhere in Internet Explorer?

Yes. To add a History list entry to your Favorites, drag it to the Favorites bar. To create an alias for a History list entry on your desktop, drag the entry to the desktop.

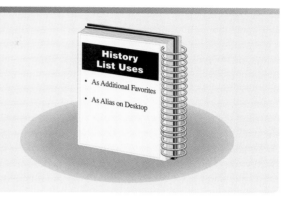

History List Uses

• As Additional Favorites

• As Alias on Desktop

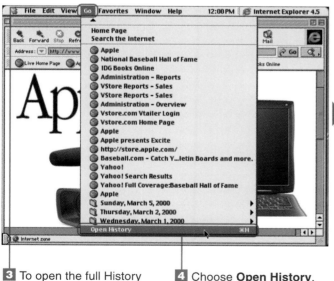

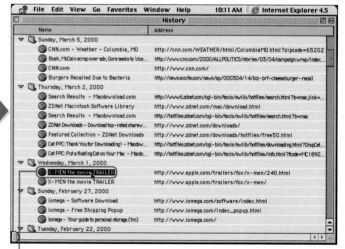

3 To open the full History list, click Go.

4 Choose **Open History**.

5 To return to a page in the History list, click it.

COPY MATERIAL FROM THE WEB

You can copy the entire contents of a Web page to your Clipboard for use in another application.

COPY MATERIAL FROM THE WEB

1 Load the page you want to copy.

2 Click **Edit**.

3 Choose **Select All**.

I want to copy just an image. How do I do it?

First, move the cursor on top of the image. Hold down the Control key and click the image, and then choose Download Image to Disk from the contextual menu.

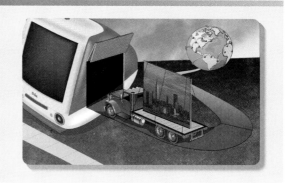

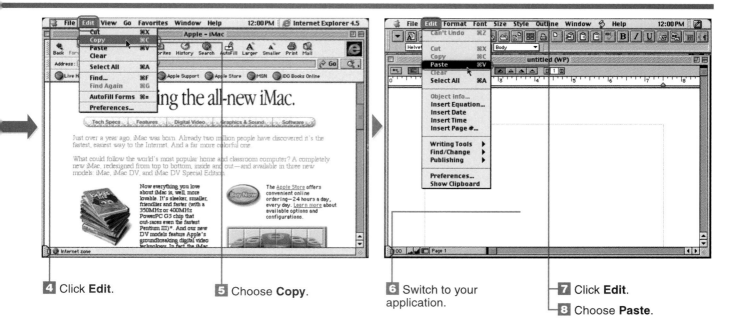

4 Click **Edit**.

5 Choose **Copy**.

6 Switch to your application.

7 Click **Edit**.

8 Choose **Paste**.

PRINT A WEB PAGE

Internet Explorer can print the contents of the a Web page.

PRINT A WEB PAGE

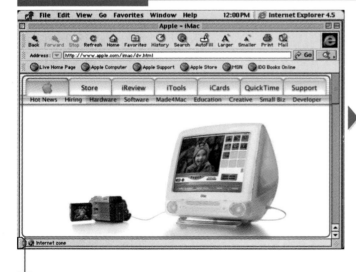

1 Load the page you want to print.

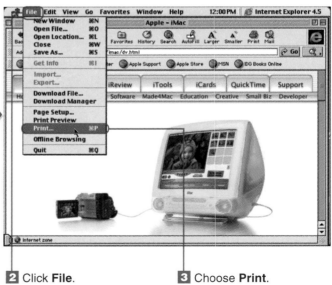

2 Click **File**.

3 Choose **Print**.

**The Web page I printed has a
background color that makes it
hard to read. How can I fix this?**

Before you print, click **File** and
choose **Print Preview**. Here, you
can specify whether to print the
contents with or without the page's
background (and whether to print
the images on the page as well as
the text).

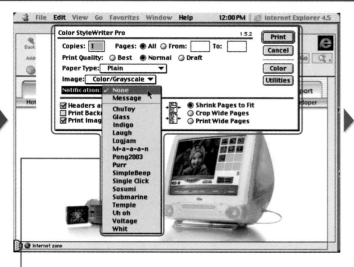

4 Make any changes
required in the Print dialog
box.

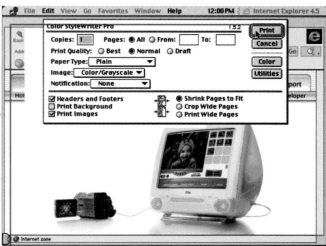

5 Click **Print**.

FROM: T. Roth
115 N. Shortridge Road
Plainville, IN 46219

TO: Yuri Yevlenko
110 Drzhinsky Plaza
Moscow

CHAPTER 10

Working with E-Mail

There's more to the Internet than just the Web. In this chapter, you find out how to send e-mail using Microsoft Outlook Express.

LAUNCH AND QUIT OUTLOOK EXPRESS

To launch and quit
Outlook Express, follow
these steps.

LAUNCH AND QUIT OUTLOOK EXPRESS

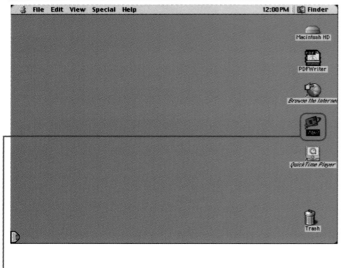

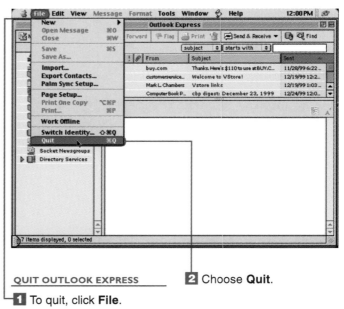

LAUNCH OUTLOOK EXPRESS

1 Double-click the Mail icon
on your desktop to open
Outlook Express.

■ If you don't have a Mail
icon on your desktop,
navigate to the Outlook
Express application on your
hard drive.

QUIT OUTLOOK EXPRESS

1 To quit, click **File**.

2 Choose **Quit**.

Here are the essential parts of the Outlook Express interface.

Button Bar

Displays common e-mail functions.

Find Button

Click the **Find** button to search for specific text in your messages.

Folder List

A convenient method of moving between standard e-mail folders (such as the Inbox and Sent Items) and newsgroup accounts.

Personal Folders

You can also set up personal folders to organize your messages.

Address Book

Click here to open your e-mail.

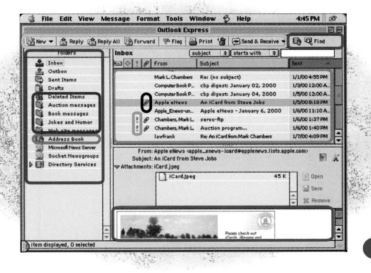

Message List Window

Displays the messages in the current folder. Click once on a message to read it. It can be resized for folders with more messages.

Preview Pane

Allows you to read a message without opening a new window. It can be resized.

Priority Icon

Indicates that the message was sent with a high priority.

File Attachment

If a message contains a **file attachment**, a paperclip icon appears here.

CONFIGURE E-MAIL SETTINGS

You must create an
Outlook Express
account to store
information, such as
your e-mail address and
preferences.

CONFIGURE E-MAIL SETTINGS

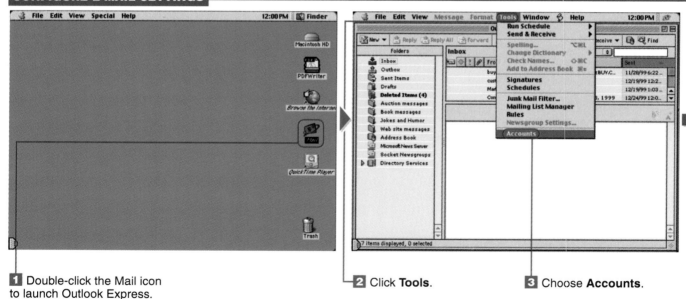

1 Double-click the Mail icon
to launch Outlook Express.

2 Click **Tools**.

3 Choose **Accounts**.

Why set up more than one account?

If others use your computer and receive e-mail with a different address (or if you receive mail from more than one e-mail address), you need multiple accounts.

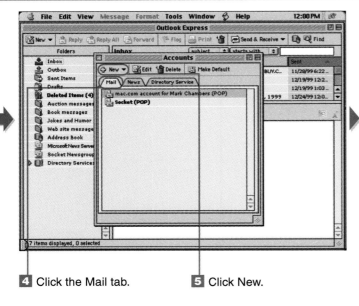

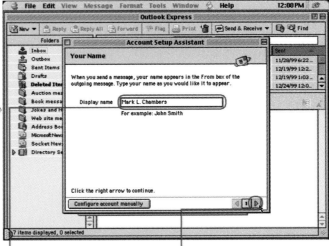

4 Click the Mail tab.

5 Click New.

6 Enter your full name as it should appear in the From: line of your messages and posts.

7 Click the right arrow to continue.

CONTINUED

CONFIGURE E-MAIL SETTINGS

Your account also contains information supplied by your Internet service provider.

Fill in your domain name below:

www.maran.com

CONFIGURE E-MAIL SETTINGS

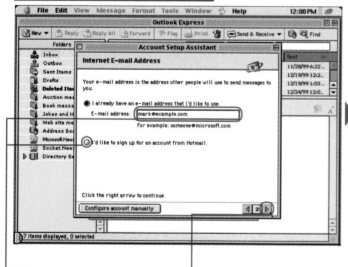

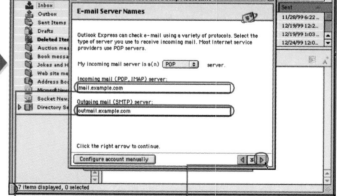

8 If you have an existing e-mail account, enter your e-mail address here.

9 To set up a free account with Hotmail, click to sign up for a Hotmail account and skip to Step 13.

10 Click the right arrow to continue.

11 Enter the mail server names provided by your ISP for your incoming and outgoing mail.

12 Click the right arrow to continue.

I don't want Outlook Express to automatically log me on. How can I protect my password?

For greater security, you can leave the password field blank while setting up the account to prevent an automatic logon. Outlook Express prompts you for your password each time you connect.

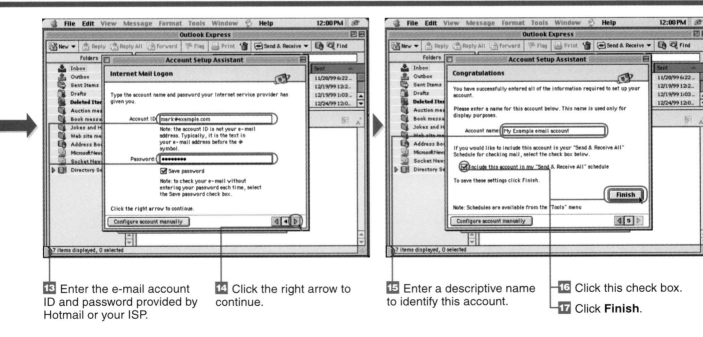

13 Enter the e-mail account ID and password provided by Hotmail or your ISP.

14 Click the right arrow to continue.

15 Enter a descriptive name to identify this account.

16 Click this check box.

17 Click **Finish**.

CHECK FOR NEW MESSAGES

After you set up your e-mail account, you are ready to check for new mail and send any mail stored in your Outbox.

CHECK FOR NEW MESSAGES

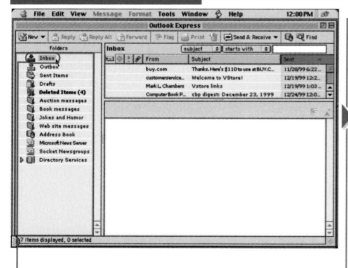

1 Click the Inbox folder to display your Inbox.

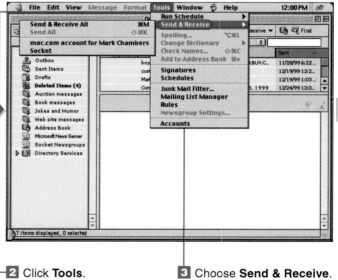

2 Click **Tools**.

3 Choose **Send & Receive**.

Are there shortcuts for the Send & Receive function?

You can also click the Send & Receive button on the toolbar or use the ⌘+M keyboard shortcut.

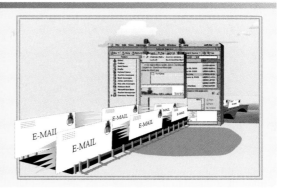

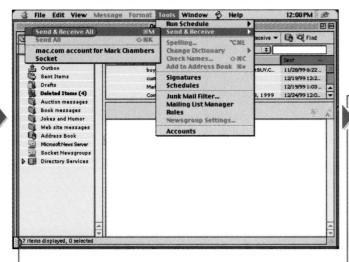

4 Click **Send & Receive All**.

5 Double-click the message in the Inbox to read it.

READ AND PRINT MESSAGES

After you receive a
message from someone,
you can preview it, read
it, or print it.

READ AND PRINT MESSAGES

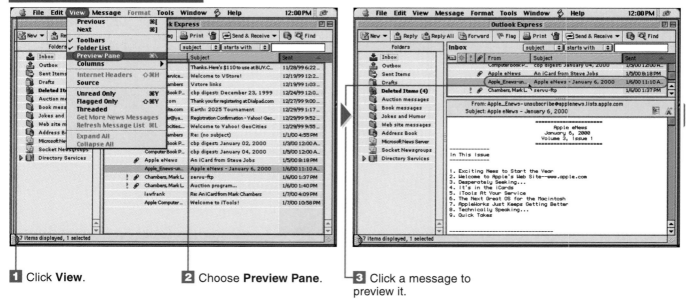

1 Click **View**.

2 Choose **Preview Pane**.

3 Click a message to
preview it.

Do I have to actually open a message before I delete it?

No. You can delete a message immediately upon receiving it (a handy feature for those who receive a great deal of junk e-mail).

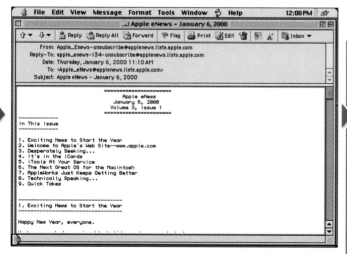

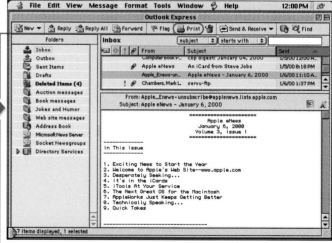

4 Double-click the message to open a new window with the message inside.

5 To print a message, click the Print button.

OPEN ATTACHMENTS

Messages that contain
attachments have the
paperclip Attachment
icon in the message list.

OPEN ATTACHMENTS

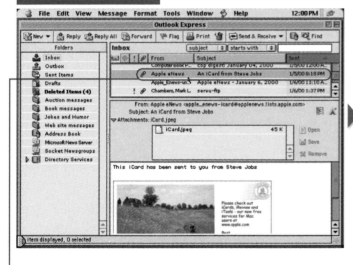

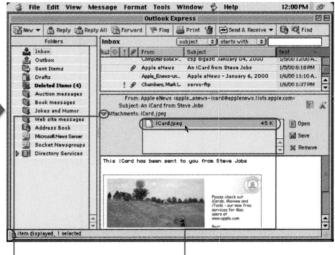

1 Click once on the
message.

2 Click the triangle next to
Attachments.

3 Click the attachment you
want to open.

How can I delete an attachment?

You can save space on your hard drive by deleting large attachments. Simply delete the message and the attachment is deleted as well.

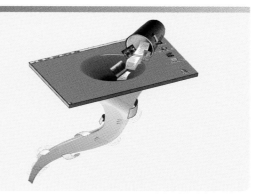

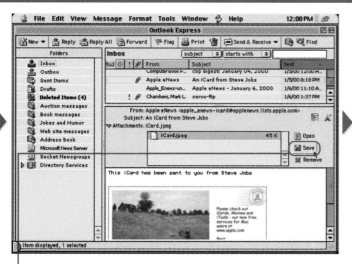

4 Click Save to save the attached file to your iMac's hard drive.

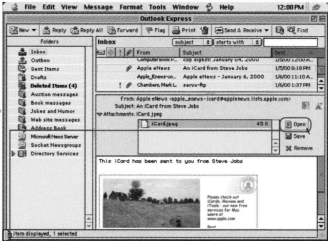

5 Click Open to run the corresponding application and open the file.

CREATE A NEW MESSAGE

You can create an
original message within
Outlook Express and
send it to one or more
recipients.

CREATE A NEW MESSAGE

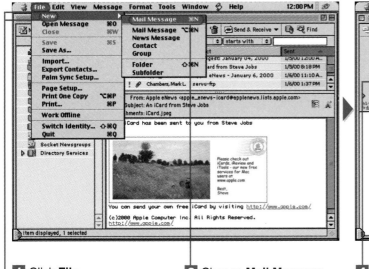

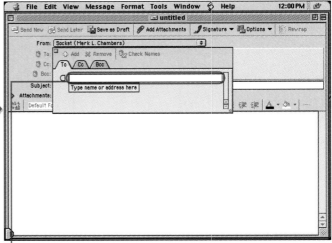

1 Click **File**.

2 Choose **New**.

3 Choose **Mail Message**.

4 Enter the recipient's
e-mail address.

5 If a matching address
from your Address Book
appears, click the desired
address to select it.

Do I have to send the message immediately?

If you don't want to connect at this time, click Send Later to send the message during the next connection Outlook Express makes to the Internet. Or click Save as Draft to save your message within the Drafts folder if you're not ready to send it.

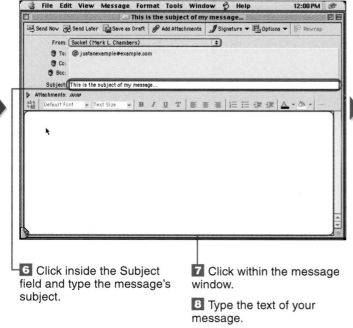

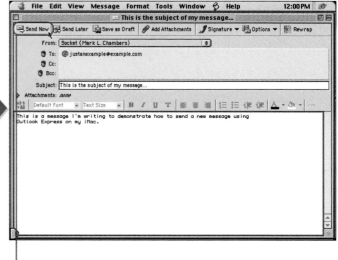

6 Click inside the Subject field and type the message's subject.

7 Click within the message window.

8 Type the text of your message.

9 Click Send Now to send the message immediately.

■ Outlook Express automatically connects to the Internet, if necessary.

REPLY TO A MESSAGE

You can reply to a
message and include the
text of the original
message.

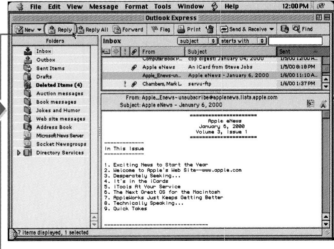

REPLY TO A MESSAGE

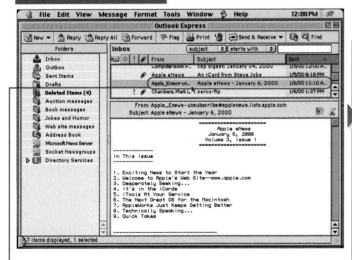

1 Click once on the desired
message in your Inbox to
highlight it.

2 Click the Reply button.

How do I reply to all the recipients of the original message?

Click Reply All to reply to the sender and other recipients of the original message.

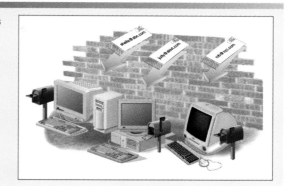

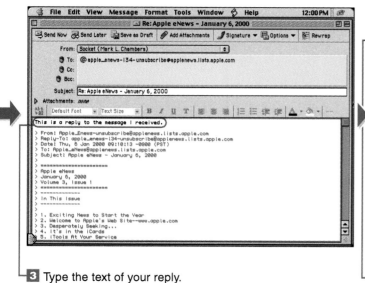

3 Type the text of your reply.

4 Click Send Now to send it immediately.

ATTACH A FILE TO A MESSAGE

Need to send one or more documents to someone across the Internet? You can attach those files to an e-mail message!

ATTACH A FILE TO A MESSAGE

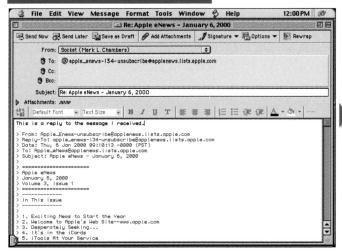

1 Create a new message or reply to an existing message in your Inbox.

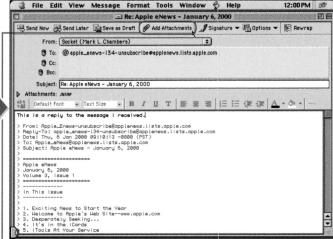

2 Click the Add Attachments button.

How big an attachment can I send?

The maximum attachment size for a message is determined by the recipient's ISP, which may place a limit on the size of an e-mail message. The larger the total size of the files you attach to a message, the longer the message takes to send.

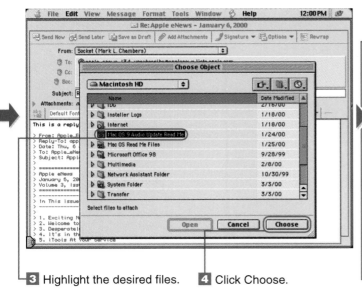

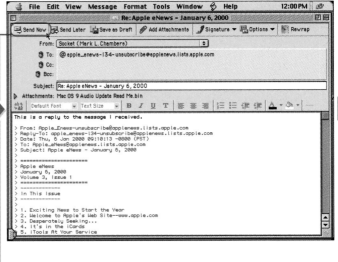

3 Highlight the desired files.   **4** Click Choose.

5 Click Send Now.

SEND CARBON COPIES

With the carbon copy feature (abbreviated CC), you can send the same message to multiple recipients.

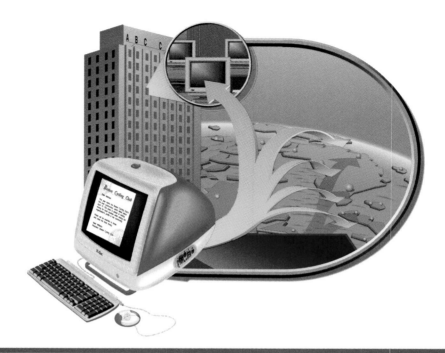

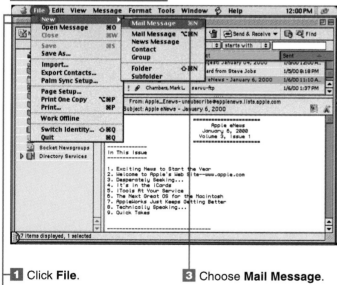

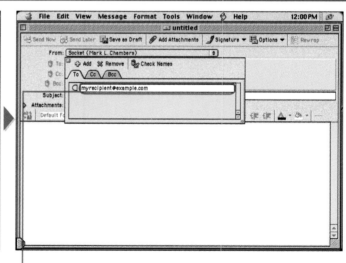

1 Click **File**.

2 Choose **New**.

3 Choose **Mail Message**.

4 Enter the recipient's e-mail address.

What's the difference between a carbon copy and a blind carbon copy?

In a regular **carbon copy** message, the main recipient in the To field also see the names and e-mail address of those in the CC: field. However, in a **blind carbon copy** (abbreviated as BCC) message, the main recipient does not see those names and e-mail addresses listed in the BCC: field.

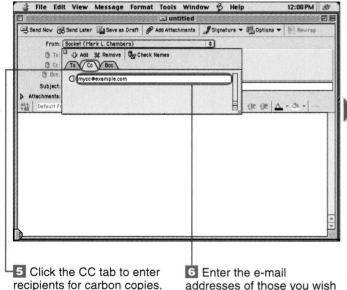

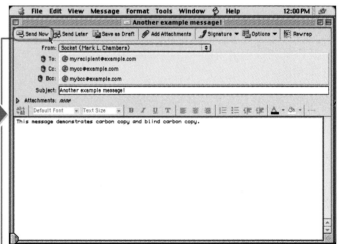

5 Click the CC tab to enter recipients for carbon copies.

■ You can also send blind carbon copies by clicking the BCC tab.

6 Enter the e-mail addresses of those you wish to receive copies of the message.

7 Click Send Now after typing in your message.

FORWARD MESSAGES

You can use the Forward feature to send a message that you received to another recipient.

Forward to:
Jim Berry

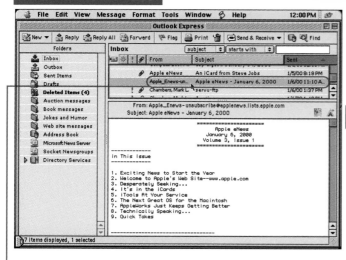

1 Click the message to highlight it.

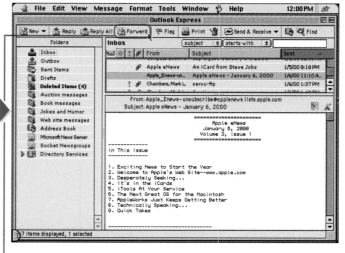

2 Click Forward.

Who becomes the sender for a forwarded message?

When you forward a message, your e-mail address is listed in the From: field.

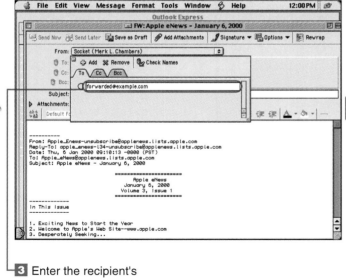

3 Enter the recipient's e-mail address.

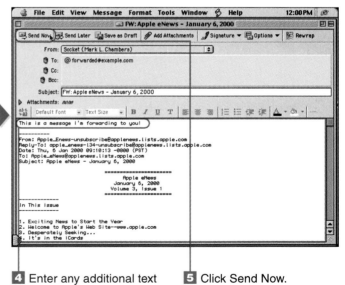

4 Enter any additional text you want to add.

5 Click Send Now.

CHAPTER 11

Using Sherlock 2

Sherlock 2 is your detective for finding documents on your hard drive and information on the Web. This chapter explains how to get the most out of your searching.

SEARCH THE WEB WITH SHERLOCK 2

Sherlock 2 (available only in Mac OS 9 and later) makes searching for Web sites and other information easy.

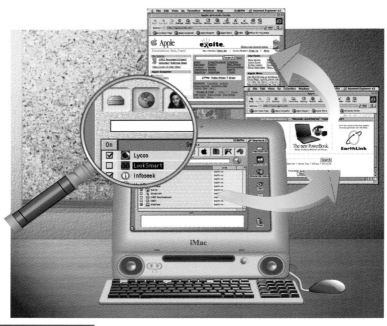

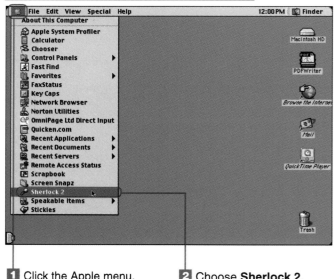

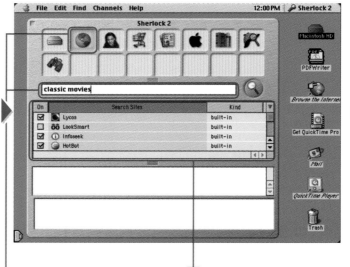

1 Click the Apple menu.

2 Choose **Sherlock 2**.

■ The Sherlock 2 main window appears.

3 Click the Internet icon.

4 Type one or more words to search for.

5 Click the appropriate check boxes (☐) for the search sites that you want Sherlock 2 to use.

Note: You may have to use the scrollbar to see all the search sites.

How do I know which sites have the most useful information?

Click **Relevance** in the site listing to sort the Web sites by their relevance to your search words.

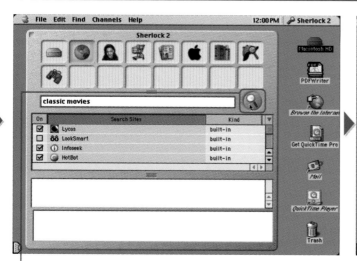

6 Click the magnifying glass icon to begin the search.

7 Click once on a site to display a short description.

8 Double-click on a site to load it within your Web browser.

SELECT A CHANNEL

You can choose an Internet channel to explore from the top of the Sherlock 2 main screen.

CHANNELS
1) Lycos
2) Yahoo!
3) **Smithsonian**
4) Discovery Channel
5) AltaVista
6) Apple

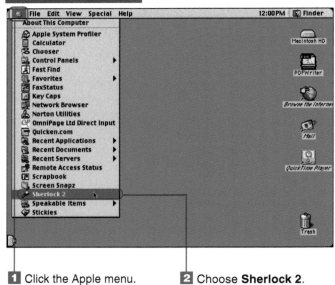

1 Click the Apple menu.

2 Choose **Sherlock 2**.

■ The Sherlock 2 main window appears.

3 Click the resizing handle  ( ) under the channel display and drag the mouse up or down to contract or expand the channel display.

4 Click the resizing handle ( ) at the lower-right corner of the Sherlock 2 window and drag to resize the window.

What is the difference between an Internet channel and a System channel?

An Internet channel searches content from Web sites on the Internet; a System channel searches the hard drive, CD-ROM, and removable media drives on your iMac.

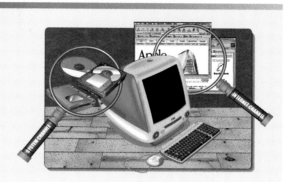

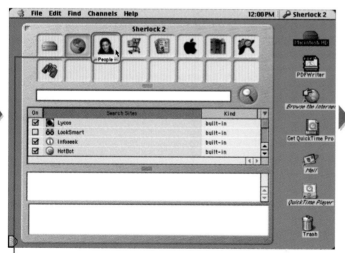

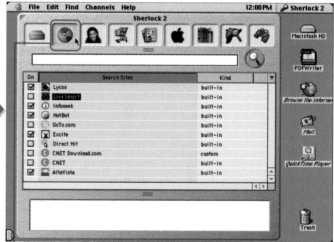

5 To display the name of a channel, rest the mouse cursor on top of the icon.

■ You can also select a channel by clicking **Channels** on the menu bar and choosing the desired channel at the bottom of the menu.

6 Click a channel to select it.

■ The corresponding search fields appear in the middle of the Sherlock 2 window.

CREATE A SHERLOCK 2 INTERNET CHANNEL

You can create your own
Sherlock 2 channels that
access your favorite
Internet search sites.

CREATE A SHERLOCK 2 INTERNET CHANNEL

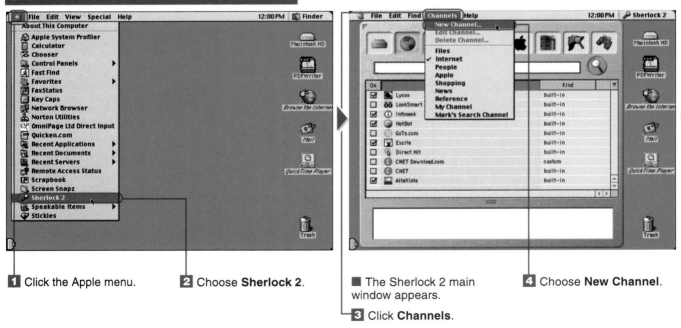

1 Click the Apple menu.

2 Choose **Sherlock 2**.

■ The Sherlock 2 main
window appears.

3 Click **Channels**.

4 Choose **New Channel**.

How can I edit or remove a channel?

Click the channel to select it. Click **Channels.** Choose **Edit Channel** or **Delete Channel.** You cannot, however, delete the default channels provided by Apple as part of Sherlock 2.

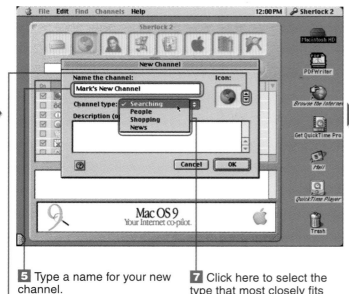

5 Type a name for your new channel.

6 Select an icon for your new channel by clicking the arrows next to the icon.

7 Click here to select the type that most closely fits your new channel.

Note: You can drag an image file on top of the Icon frame to use a custom image.

8 Type a description of the channel to help you identify it.

9 Click **OK** to save your new channel.

FIND FILES ON YOUR HARD DRIVE

Need to find a file
somewhere on your
iMac's hard drive? If you
know all or part of its
name, you can use
Sherlock 2 to find it.

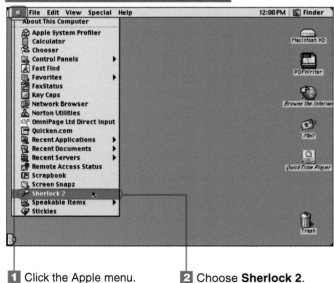

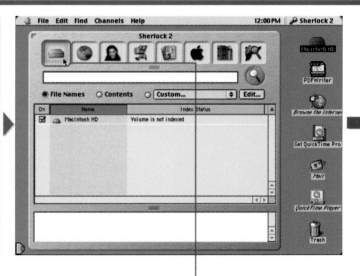

1 Click the Apple menu.

2 Choose **Sherlock 2**.

■ The Sherlock 2 main
window appears.

3 Click the Files channel
icon.

How can I determine where the file is?

Click once on a file entry and Sherlock 2 displays the file's location in the middle section of the window.

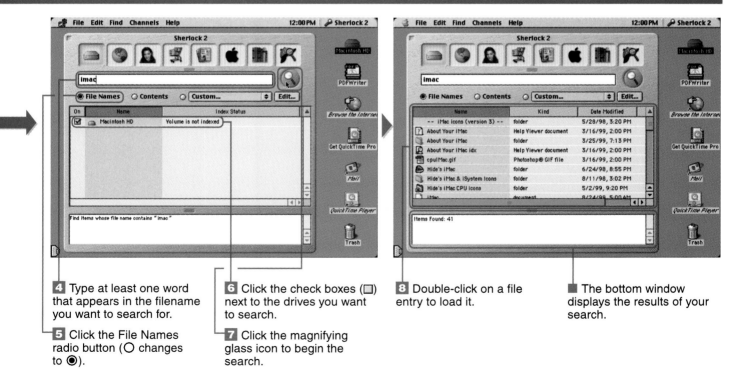

4 Type at least one word that appears in the filename you want to search for.

5 Click the File Names radio button (○ changes to ◉).

6 Click the check boxes (☐) next to the drives you want to search.

7 Click the magnifying glass icon to begin the search.

8 Double-click on a file entry to load it.

■ The bottom window displays the results of your search.

CREATE A VOLUME INDEX

Sherlock 2 enables you to search for specific content within the files on your system. However, you must create a volume index first.

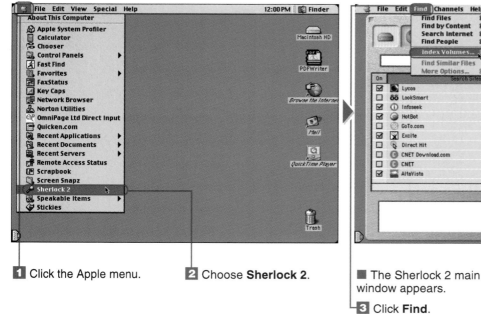

1 Click the Apple menu.

2 Choose **Sherlock 2**.

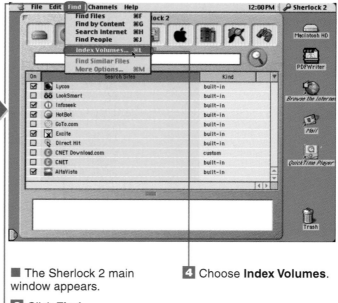

■ The Sherlock 2 main window appears.

3 Click **Find**.

4 Choose **Index Volumes**.

248

How often should I index my files?

At least once a month, depending on how often you add new files or edit your documents.

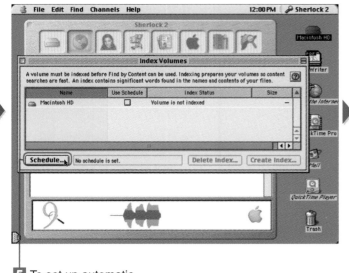

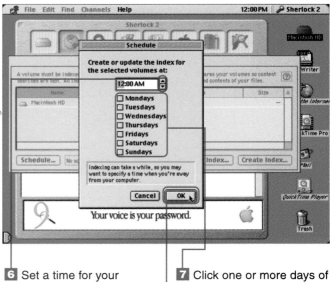

5 To set up automatic indexing on a regular basis, click **Schedule**.

6 Set a time for your scheduled index update by clicking the arrows.

7 Click one or more days of the week to add them to the schedule.

8 Click **OK**.

CONTINUED

CREATE A VOLUME INDEX

After you set a schedule (if desired), you can begin the actual indexing process.

CREATE A VOLUME INDEX

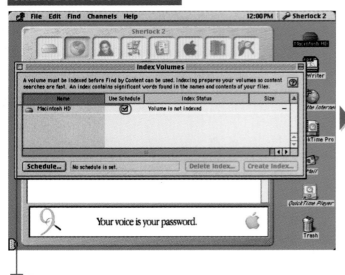

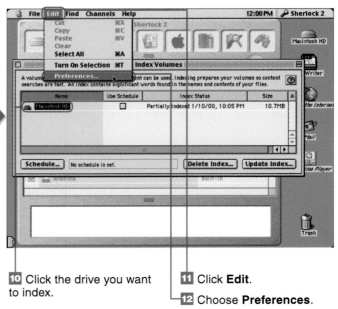

9 To use a schedule that you previously set up, click the Use Schedule check box (☐) next to the desired drives.

10 Click the drive you want to index.

11 Click **Edit**.

12 Choose **Preferences**.

Can I speed up the index process?

From the Preferences dialog box, move the System responsiveness slider to the right. You can also reduce the amount of indexing by clicking **Languages** and deselecting all the languages that do not appear in your files.

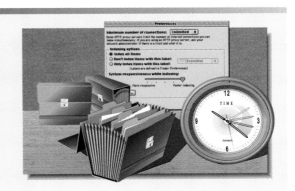

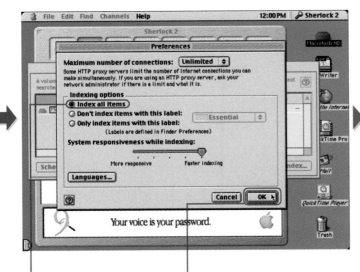

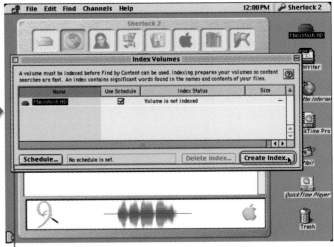

13 For the most thorough search, click this radio button to index all items (○ changes to ◉).

■ You can selectively index files with a certain label to save time, or you can omit items by a label you choose.

14 Click **OK**.

15 Click **Create Index** to begin.

FIND CONTENT

After you create a volume index, you can use Sherlock 2 to search the data within the files on your drive for specific words or phrases.

Creating a volume index is discussed earlier in this chapter.

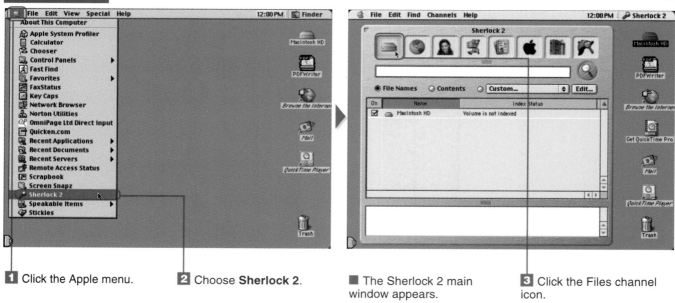

1 Click the Apple menu.

2 Choose **Sherlock 2**.

■ The Sherlock 2 main window appears.

3 Click the Files channel icon.

**Do I have to enter the search
criteria each time I use Sherlock 2?**

If you are going to search several
times using specific criteria, you
can save your search criteria in a
file and load it each time. Click **File.**
Choose **Save Search Criteria.**
Alternately, you can create a
custom search (as shown in the
next section) and save it to disk.

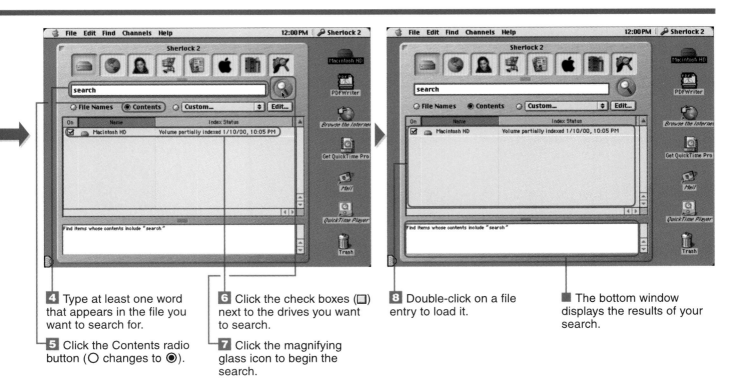

4 Type at least one word
that appears in the file you
want to search for.

5 Click the Contents radio
button (○ changes to ◉).

6 Click the check boxes (□)
next to the drives you want
to search.

7 Click the magnifying
glass icon to begin the
search.

8 Double-click on a file
entry to load it.

■ The bottom window
displays the results of your
search.

CREATE A CUSTOM SEARCH

You can combine the different types of searches covered in this chapter to create a powerful *custom search* based on more than one type of criteria — for example, content, filename, and file type.

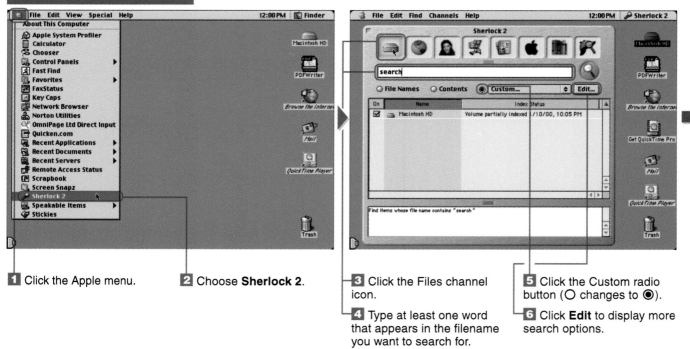

1 Click the Apple menu.

2 Choose **Sherlock 2**.

3 Click the Files channel icon.

4 Type at least one word that appears in the filename you want to search for.

5 Click the Custom radio button (O changes to ●).

6 Click **Edit** to display more search options.

Do I need to enter all the custom search criteria?

No, only the values you enable by clicking the check box next to the field name. If you do not check a field, Sherlock 2 does not use it.

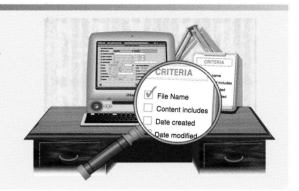

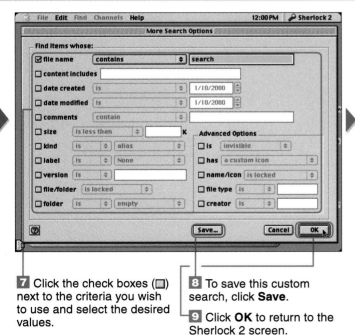

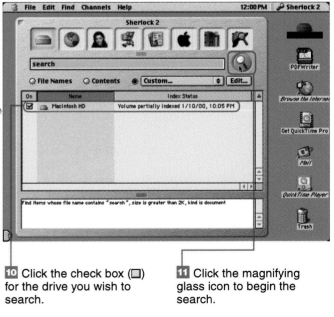

7 Click the check boxes (☐) next to the criteria you wish to use and select the desired values.

8 To save this custom search, click **Save**.

9 Click **OK** to return to the Sherlock 2 screen.

10 Click the check box (☐) for the drive you wish to search.

11 Click the magnifying glass icon to begin the search.

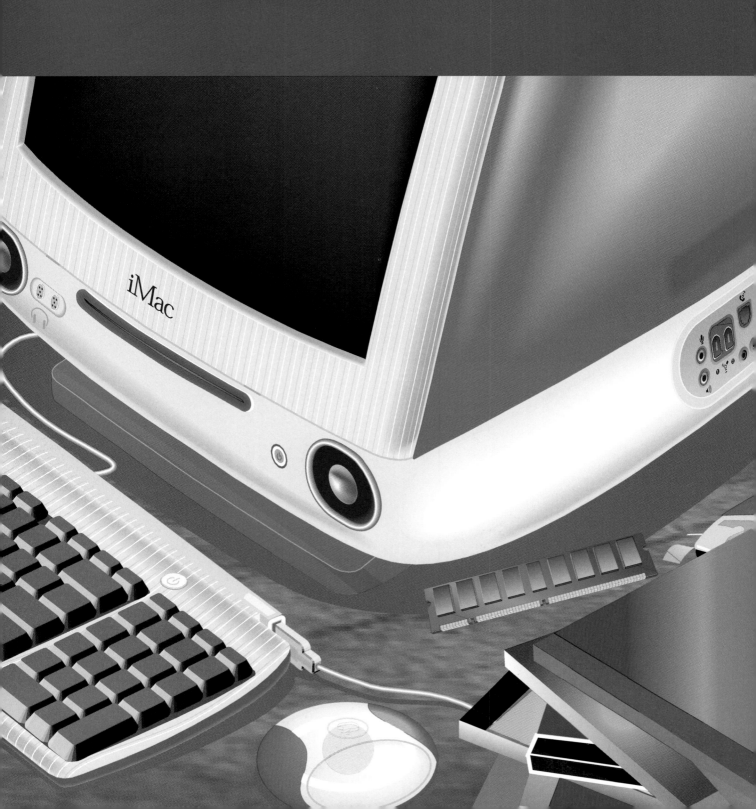

CHAPTER 12

Upgrading Your iMac

Your iMac is very versatile. This chapter shows you how to add all kinds of toys to your iMac.

ADD EXTERNAL SPEAKERS

Although the built-in speakers on your iMac are fine for typical home use, audio enthusiasts and game players may want to add external speakers.

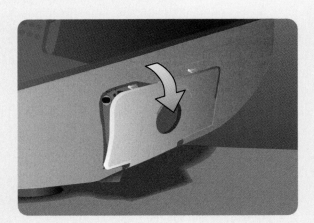

1 If you have an older iMac with an access door covering the ports, open the door by pulling on the finger hole.

Note: If you have a new iMac, there is no access door; the ports are open.

2 If your iMac has an access door, run the cable from your external speakers through one of the cutouts in the door.

What type of external speakers are best?

If you're a dedicated gamer or music lover, choose a speaker system with a *subwoofer*. The low-frequency bass it produces improves the sound of your compact discs and adds realism to sound effects.

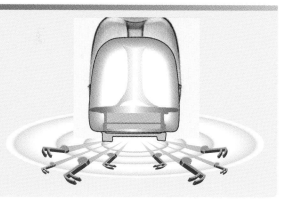

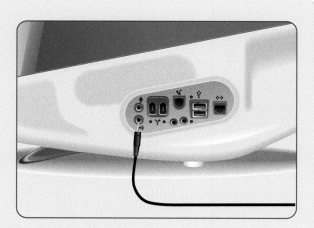

3 Push the connector on the speaker cable into the speaker jack on your iMac.

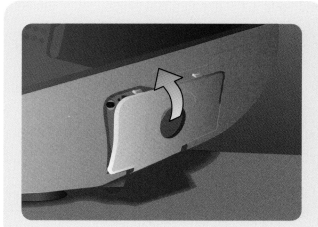

4 Close the access door, if necessary.

ADD USB PERIPHERALS

You can upgrade and expand your iMac with a number of USB peripherals.

ADD USB PERIPHERALS

1 If you have an older iMac with an access door, open it by pulling on the fingerhole.

Note: If you have a new iMac, there is no access door; the ports are open.

2 If necessary, feed the USB cable from the device through one of the cutouts in the access door.

Can I plug a USB device into the second iMac keyboard port?

Because your mouse uses only one USB port on your keyboard, you can plug a USB device into the second port. However, the USB device must have its own power supply and should not draw power from the USB cable.

3 Install any required driver software and reboot your iMac.

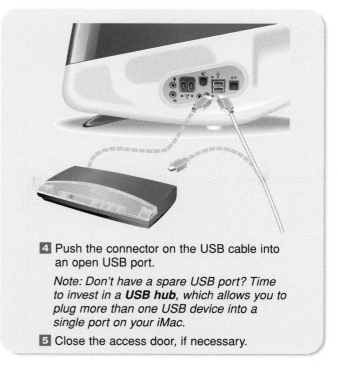

4 Push the connector on the USB cable into an open USB port.

*Note: Don't have a spare USB port? Time to invest in a **USB hub**, which allows you to plug more than one USB device into a single port on your iMac.*

5 Close the access door, if necessary.

ADD RAM

You can easily install additional random access memory (RAM) in your system.

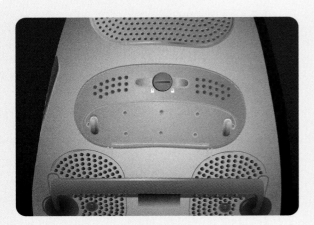

1 Locate the system RAM upgrade panel at the back of your iMac.

Note: If your iMac is an older model, you have to open the case to add RAM. I recommend that a RAM upgrade be installed professionally at an authorized Apple service center.

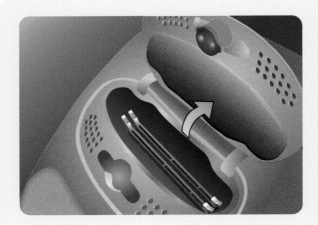

2 Remove the cover to expose the upgrade slot.

Can I install the RAM module the wrong way?

Because of the notches in the module, you can install a RAM module only the right way! However, make sure that you seat the gold connectors firmly in the socket before you press down so that proper contact is made between the module and the socket.

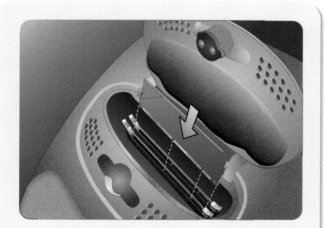

3 Align the tabs in the upgrade slot with the notches in the RAM module.

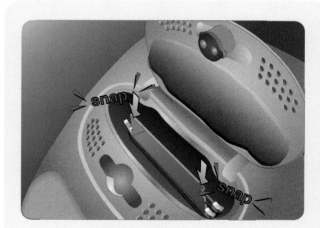

4 Push the RAM module into the upgrade slot at an angle until it's firmly seated in the slot.

5 Press down on the module until it clicks into place.

6 Replace the cover panel.

UPGRADE YOUR HARD DRIVE

If you need additional space to store more programs and data, you have several options.

You can replace the existing hard drive in your iMac with a larger hard drive. I recommend that a new hard drive be installed professionally at an authorized Apple service center.

Note: If you replace your existing drive, you have to back up and restore all your existing programs and data.

You can add more storage space with an external USB hard drive. Follow the steps in "Adding USB Peripherals" earlier in this chapter.

Does an external drive replace my existing internal hard drive?

No. The external drive simply provides additional space, and it appears as a separate drive icon on your desktop.

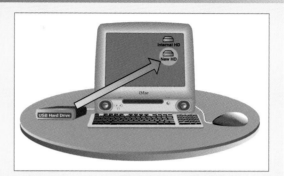

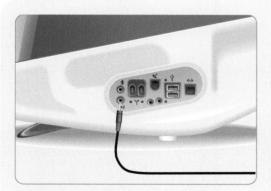

If you have a new iMac, a FireWire hard drive is the fastest external storage solution. FireWire also allows you to connect a digital video camera to your iMac.

Note: Make sure that you install all the FireWire drivers and system extensions before connecting your drive. Check your drive's manual for more information.

You can also add an external USB or FireWire CD recorder, which can permanently store up to 750MB of data on a single CD-ROM.

UPGRADE THE MAC OS

If your iMac shipped with an earlier version of the Mac OS — for example, Mac OS 8.6 — you can add functionality by upgrading to the latest version.

Note: Although installing future versions of the Mac OS may differ slightly, these general steps should help you.

UPGRADE THE MAC OS

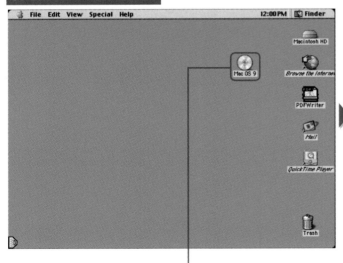

1 Load the Mac OS CD-ROM into your CD-ROM drive.

2 Open the CD-ROM.

3 Double-click the Mac OS Install icon.

4 Click **Continue**.

What is a clean install?

A *clean install* reinstalls the operating system in a new System Folder, renaming your old System Folder. You can move any third-party extensions and Control Panels from the old System Folder to the new one. Perform a clean install only if your computer is experiencing serious trouble or if directed by Apple Tech Support.

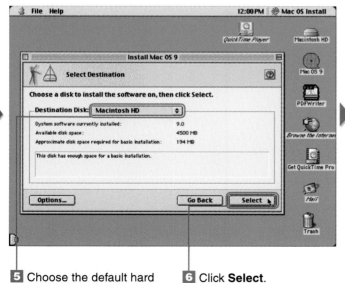

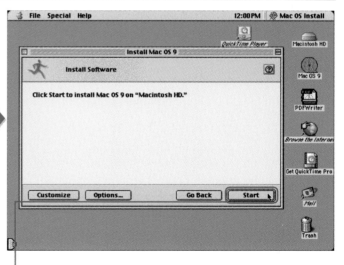

5 Choose the default hard drive as the destination for the software.

6 Click **Select**.

Note: You need to read the Before You Install information and accept the User License Agreement.

7 Click **Start** to begin the installation.

UPGRADE THE IMAC FIRMWARE

Your iMac uses *firmware* to control many of the basic functions — for example, sending data to and from your hard drive and monitor. From time-to-time, Apple releases upgrades for your iMac's firmware, and you should always apply these upgrades.

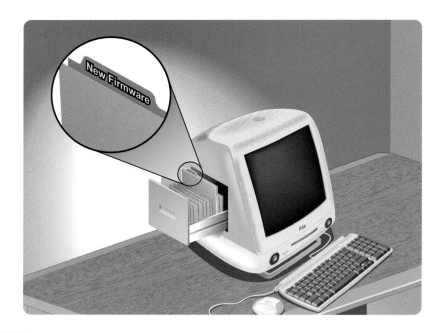

UPGRADE THE IMAC FIRMWARE

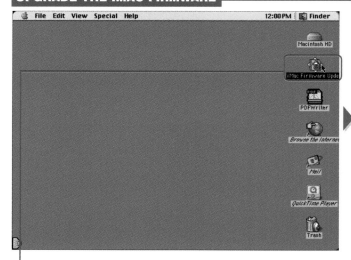

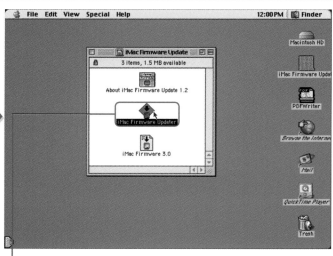

1 Open the folder containing the Firmware Updater.

2 Double-click the program icon.

3 After the firmware updates, shut down in order to complete the update process.

Will a firmware update cause problems with my programs or data?

No. Your hard drive is not affected. However, some of your Control Panel preferences return to their defaults, so you may need to set them again.

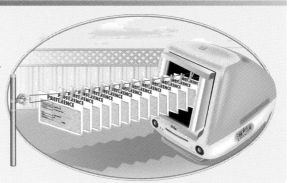

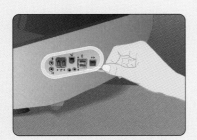

4 If necessary, open the access door on the right side of your iMac.

5 Push the end of a straightened paper clip gently into the Reset hole.

6 As you hold the paper clip in the hole, turn on your iMac by pressing the Power button.

■ Your iMac will emits a long tone to indicate that you can remove the paper clip.

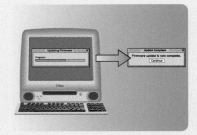

7 The updated firmware automatically loads itself, indicated by a progress bar on the screen.

8 Your iMac displays a confirmation message after the update has successfully completed.

CHAPTER 13

Optimizing Your iMac

Your iMac runs pretty well out of the box, but you can make it run even better. This chapter gives you tips and tricks on optimizing your iMac's performance.

CREATE A RAM DISK

A RAM disk is a *virtual* hard drive created with your iMac's system RAM; programs run faster and data can be accessed faster when stored on a RAM disk.

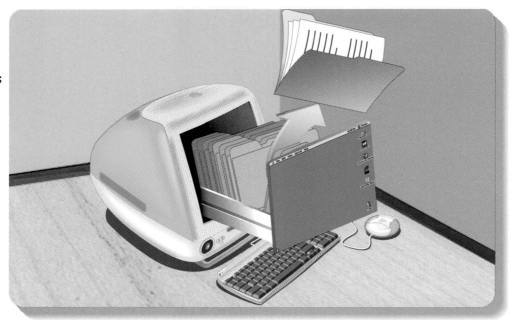

CREATE A RAM DISK

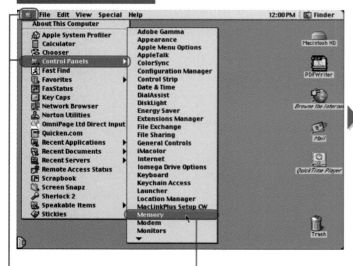

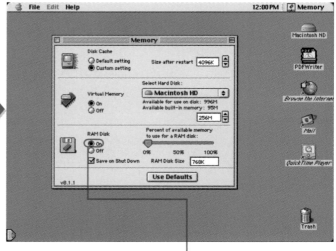

1 Click the Apple menu.

2 Choose **Control Panels**.

3 Choose **Memory**.

■ The Memory Control Panel appears.

4 Click the On radio button to turn on the RAM disk (○ changes to ◉).

Is the data in a RAM disk safe while my iMac is off?

If you enable the Save on Shut Down feature, the data in your RAM disk is automatically saved to disk when you shut down your iMac, and it is automatically restored to the RAM disk when you start your computer. If you disable this feature, you lose the contents of your RAM disk when you shut down or restart — or if a power failure hits.

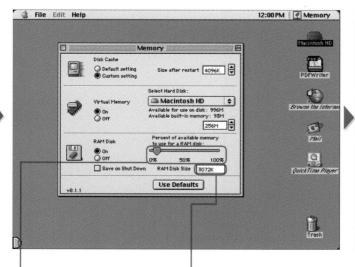

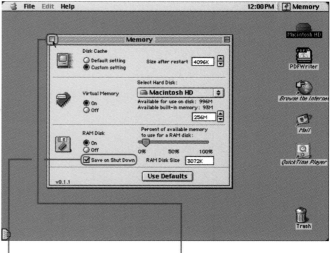

■5■ Move the slider to set the percentage of available memory to use for the RAM disk.

■ You can also click here to specify a size for the RAM disk. A 2MB RAM disk is appropriate for an iMac with 32MB of system RAM; double that figure for a system with 64MB of RAM.

■6■ Click the **Save on Shut Down** check box (☐ changes to ☑).

■7■ Click the Close box to save your changes.

USING VIRTUAL MEMORY

The Mac OS can use space on your hard drive as *virtual memory*, enabling you to run multiple programs and load large documents that you normally couldn't access with just your system RAM.

USING VIRTUAL MEMORY

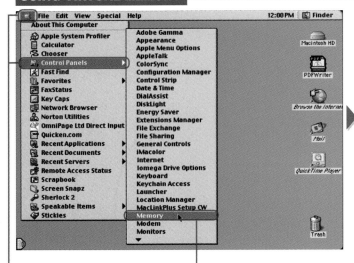

1 Click the Apple menu.

2 Choose **Control Panels**.

3 Choose **Memory**.

■ The Memory Control Panel appears.

4 Click the On radio button to turn on virtual memory (○ changes to ◉).

Why would I want to turn off virtual memory?

Your iMac runs slightly faster if you turn off virtual memory, but I recommend that you leave virtual memory on unless you have at least 128MB of system RAM.

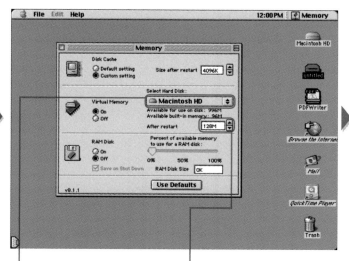

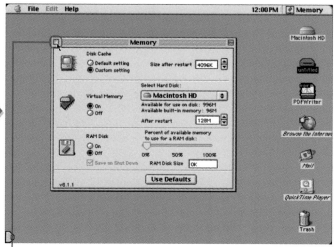

5 Select either the internal hard drive or an external drive.

6 Choose the total amount of RAM you want after restart.

Note: This total includes both the actual built-in RAM and the amount of virtual memory you allocate.

7 Click the Close box to save your changes.

8 Restart your iMac.

EXPAND THE DISK CACHE

If your iMac has at least 64MB of system RAM, expanding the size of your disk cache is a good idea. The *disk cache* holds data that is accessed often, which can help improve performance when reading and writing files.

EXPAND THE DISK CACHE

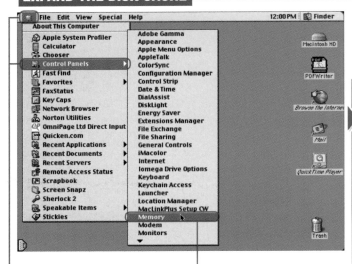

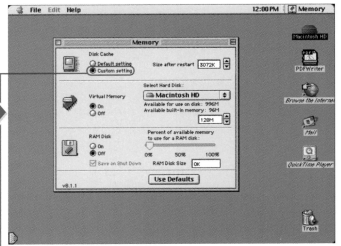

1 Click the Apple menu.

2 Choose **Control Panels**.

3 Choose **Memory**.

■ The Memory Control Panel appears.

4 Click the Custom Setting radio button (○ changes to ◉).

5 At the confirmation prompt, click **Custom** to continue.

What is a good cache size to select?

If you have 64MB of system RAM, select a cache size of 4096K. For an iMac with 128MB or more, select a cache size of 8192K.

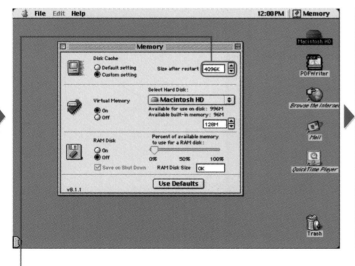

6 Choose the size of the disk cache.

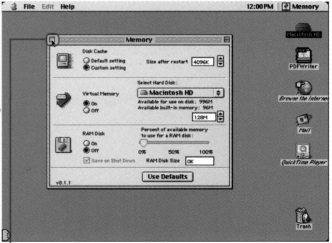

7 Click the Close box to save your changes.

8 Restart your iMac.

ALLOCATE EXTRA MEMORY TO A PROGRAM

Some Macintosh programs may require a reserve of additional memory (especially programs that work with large desktop publishing, graphics, or multimedia files). If a program advises you that it is running out of memory, try allocating additional system RAM.

ALLOCATE EXTRA MEMORY TO A PROGRAM

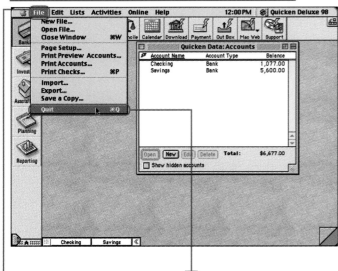

Note: You must quit the program first before you can allocate additional RAM.

1 Click **File**.

2 Choose **Quit** to exit out of the program.

3 Click the program's icon to highlight it.

4 Click **File**.

5 Choose **Get Info**.

**Why does a program need
additional memory?**

If you create or edit a large
document — for example, a digital
video clip — the program that you
are using may require additional
work space in the RAM to hold the
data.

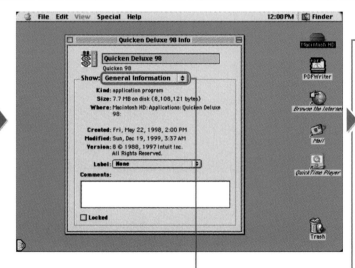

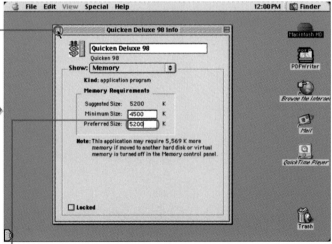

■ The program's Info dialog
box appears. This window
gives you general information
about the program.

6 Click the Show drop-down
list and choose **Memory**.

7 Click in the Preferred
Size box and enter a higher
amount of RAM.

8 Click the Close box to
save your changes.

RUN AN APPLESCRIPT TASK

By using AppleScript, you can automate common tasks that you would normally have to perform manually, such as adding an alias to the Apple menu or synchronizing the contents of two folders.

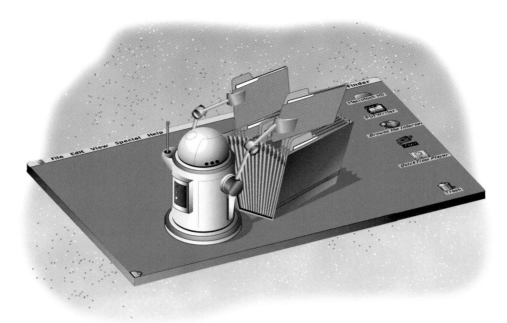

RUN AN APPLESCRIPT TASK

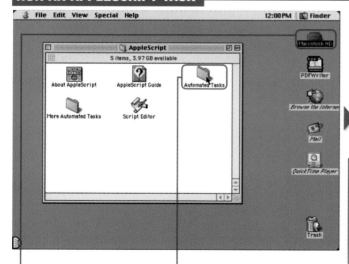

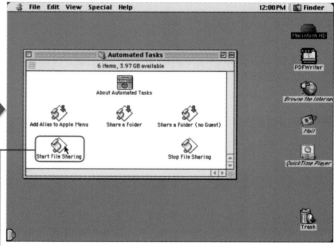

1 From the desktop, double-click the hard drive icon to open it.

2 Double-click the **Apple Extras** folder to open it.

3 Double-click the **AppleScript** folder to open it.

4 Double-click the **Automated Tasks** folder to open it.

■ The Automated Tasks window appears.

5 Double-click the desired AppleScript icon to launch the script.

Note: Depending on your version of the Mac OS, you may also have a second folder called More Automated Tasks, which contains additional scripts.

Why would I want to use a script?

Using scripts saves time. Instead of pressing keys and clicking the mouse to complete a task, the iMac combines all these manual actions and performs them automatically when you click the script.

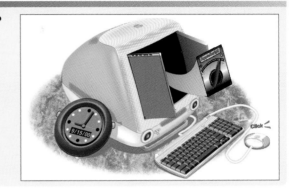

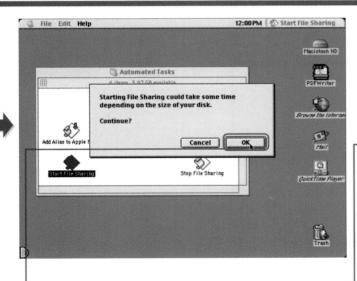

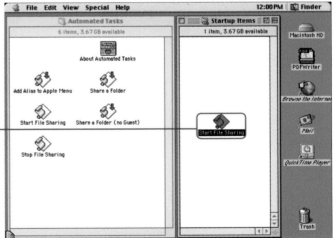

■ Some scripts confirm whether you want to continue. Click **OK** to start the script.

RUNNING A SCRIPT AUTOMATICALLY DURING STARTUP

1 Copy the script to the Startup Items folder inside your System.

Note: To copy the script, hold down the Option key while you drag.

2 Restart your iMac.

SET UP A MULTIUSER SYSTEM

If you share your iMac, you can configure Mac OS 9 as a *multiuser* system, where each person can use a unique *account*. Each account saves individual preferences for application, desktop, and view settings.

SET UP A MULTIUSER SYSTEM

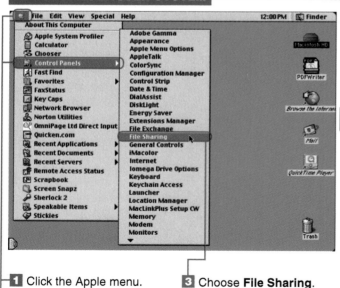

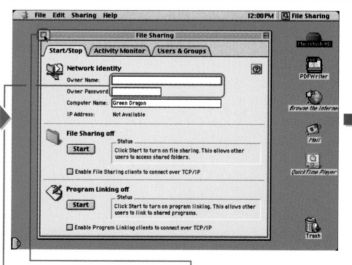

1 Click the Apple menu.

2 Choose **Control Panels**.

3 Choose **File Sharing**.

■ The File Sharing Control Panel appears.

4 If the Owner Name and Owner Password fields are empty, type a name and password.

5 Click the Close box to exit and save your changes.

Who is the Owner of a multiuser system?

The Owner account within a MacOS multiuser system is essentially the "system administrator" — the Owner has access to all functions of the computer and all the commands within the operating system.

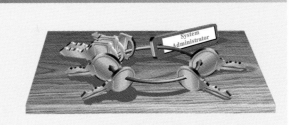

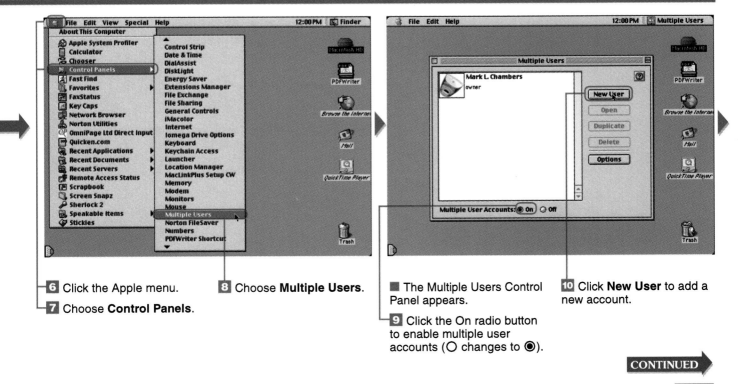

6 Click the Apple menu.

7 Choose **Control Panels**.

8 Choose **Multiple Users**.

■ The Multiple Users Control Panel appears.

9 Click the On radio button to enable multiple user accounts (O changes to ◉).

10 Click **New User** to add a new account.

CONTINUED

SET UP A MULTIUSER SYSTEM

After you have configured your iMac as a multiuser system, you can add a new account for each person who will use your computer.

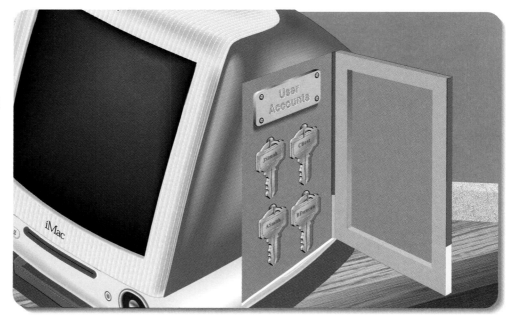

SET UP A MULTIUSER SYSTEM

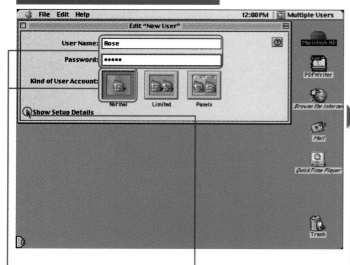

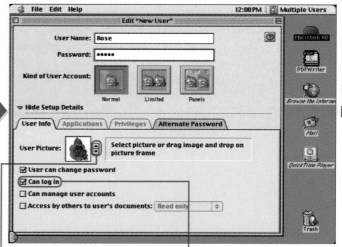

11 Type a User Name and Password for this account.

12 Click **Normal** for the level of user security.

13 Click here to show setup details.

14 Select a User Picture by using the arrows to scroll through the available options.

Note: You can drag an image file on top of the User Picture frame to use a custom image.

15 Click this check box to allow the user to log in (☐ changes to ☑).

How can I create a number of accounts with the same settings?

Create the first account, select that account on the Multiple Users Control Panel, and click **Duplicate.**

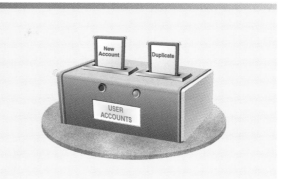

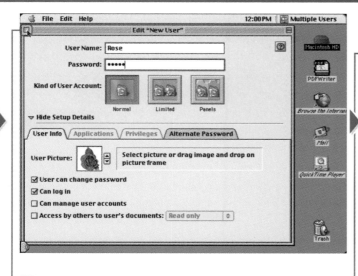

16 Click the Close box to exit and save your changes.

■ The New user appears in the Multiple Users Control Panel.

17 Click the Close box to close the Multiple Users Control Panel.

18 Restart your iMac to display the Login screen.

USING VOICEPRINT SECURITY

With *voiceprint* enabled as your alternate password, you can log in to a Mac OS 9 multiuser system by simply speaking to your iMac!

USING VOICEPRINT SECURITY

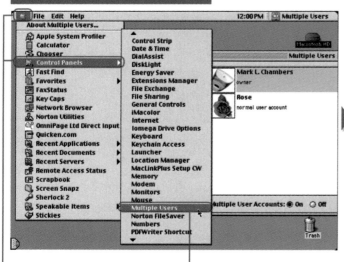

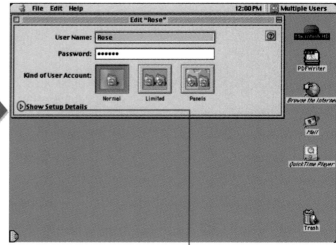

1 Log in to your iMac as the system owner.

2 Click the Apple menu.

3 Choose **Control Panels**.

4 Choose **Multiple Users**.

■ The Multiple Users Control Panel appears.

5 Double-click the desired account entry to edit it.

6 Click here to show setup details.

The Alternate Password tab is grayed out. How do I set an alternate password?

To enable alternate passwords, open the Multiple Users Control Panel and click **Options.** Click the **Login** tab and click the **Allow Alternate Password** check box.

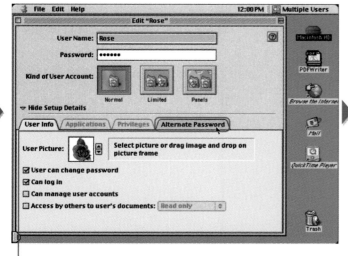

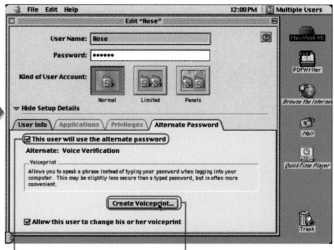

7 Click the **Alternate Password** tab.

8 Click the check box to indicate that this user will use the alternate password (☐ changes to ☑).

9 Click **Create Voiceprint.**

CONTINUED ▸

USING VOICEPRINT SECURITY

Make sure you speak the voiceprint phrase with the same volume and inflection each time to create a consistent voiceprint.

USING VOICEPRINT SECURITY

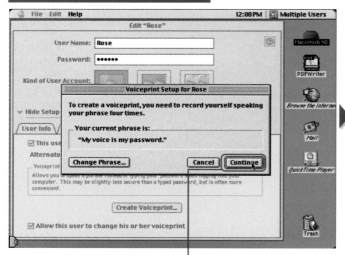

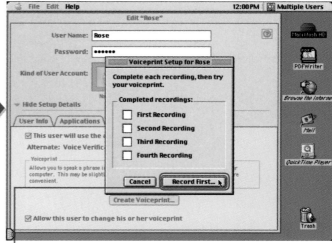

■ The Voiceprint Setup dialog box appears.

10 Click **Continue** to accept the current voiceprint phrase.

11 Click **Record First**.

How do I change the voiceprint phrase?

Click **Change Phrase** from the Voiceprint Setup dialog box and type the new phrase that your iMac will display at the Voiceprint login screen. Click **OK** to save the phrase.

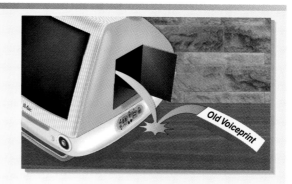

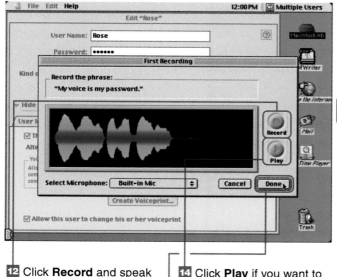

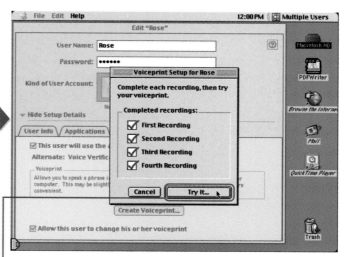

12 Click **Record** and speak the voiceprint phrase.

13 Click the **Stop** button when you finish the recording.

14 Click **Play** if you want to hear what you just recorded.

15 Click **Done** to continue.

16 Repeat Steps 11 through 15 three more times.

17 After you make all four recordings, click **Try It** to test your voiceprint.

18 Click the Close box to close the Edit User dialog box.

19 Click the Close box to close the Multiple Users Control Panel.

ASSIGN HOT FUNCTION KEYS

By setting up convenient *hot function key* assignments, you can run an application or load a document with a single key sequence.

ASSIGN HOT FUNCTION KEYS

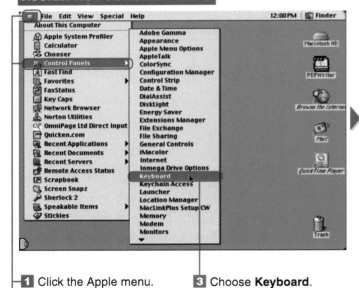

1 Click the Apple menu.

2 Choose **Control Panels**.

3 Choose **Keyboard**.

■ The Keyboard Control Panel appears.

4 Click **Function Keys**.

Will hot function keys interfere with the regular function key assignments in my applications?

No. Because you enabled the **Use F1 Through F12 As Function Keys** check box, you can use them normally (programs normally assign commands to function keys). However, you can now access the hot function keys you assigned by holding down the Option key as you press the function key.

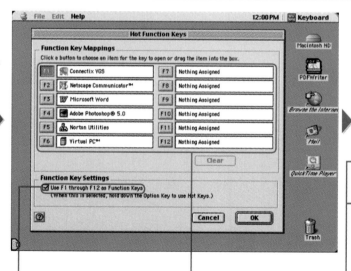

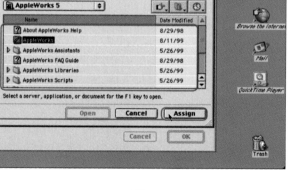

5 Click this check box, which keeps the normal functions for the F1 through F12 function keys (☐ changes to ☑).

6 Click the function key button you want to assign.

7 Locate the document or program you want to assign and select it.

8 Click **Assign**.

9 Click **OK** to exit the Hot Function Keys dialog box.

10 Click the Close box to close the Keyboard Control Panel.

CHAPTER 14

Troubleshooting Problems

Even the iMac isn't immune to common computer problems. This chapter is your guide for when things start to go wrong.

CONFIGURE AUTOMATIC SOFTWARE UPDATE

Mac OS 9 includes *automatic software updating,* which allows your iMac to automatically download updates for your system and application files from the Internet.

CONFIGURE AUTOMATIC SOFTWARE UPDATE

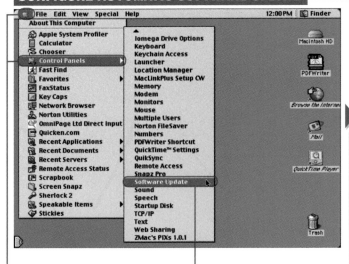

1 Click the Apple menu.

2 Click **Control Panels**.

3 Click **Software Update**.

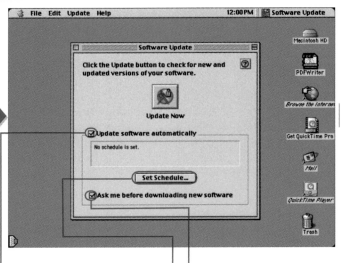

■ The Software Update Control Panel appears.

4 Click this check box to update software automatically.

5 Click this check box to receive an alert before downloading new software.

6 Click **Set Schedule** to specify an update schedule.

294

What changes are made when I update?

Typically, Apple releases updates to correct software bugs. However, some updates may actually add new functionality or updated hardware drivers to the Mac OS or an application.

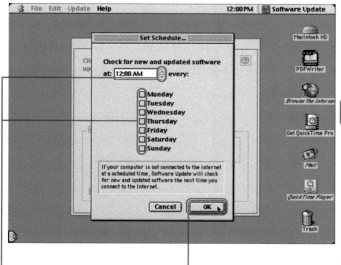

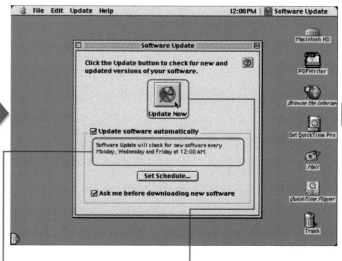

7 Use the arrows to select a time for your iMac to check for updates.

8 Click the appropriate check boxes for the days you want to check for updates.

9 Click **OK** to save your changes.

■ The schedule you selected appears in the window.

10 Click **Update Now** to immediately check for updates.

CONTINUED

CONFIGURE AUTOMATIC SOFTWARE UPDATE

Your iMac automatically applies the updates that you download, but you may have to restart your computer manually to complete the process.

CONFIGURE AUTOMATIC SOFTWARE UPDATE

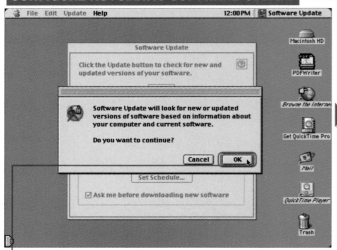

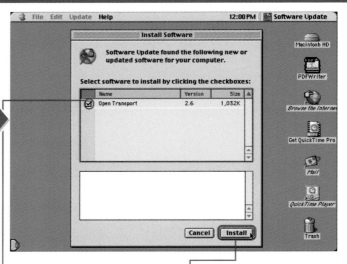

11 Click **OK** to confirm that you want to check for updates.

■ Your iMac connects to the Internet and checks for updates.

■ If your iMac finds updates, they appear in the Install Software window.

12 Click the check box next to the updates you want to download.

13 Click **Install** to begin the download process.

Note: Many updates require you to close all other programs running on your iMac. The Software Update Control Panel can do this for you automatically.

Some of these updates are very large files. How can I choose the files I want to download?

Click the Ask me before downloading new software check box, and your iMac asks you for confirmation before downloading any files.

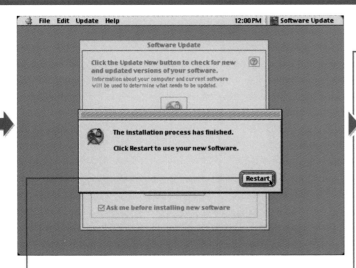

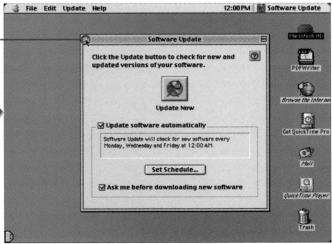

14 If necessary, click **Restart** after the download has completed.

15 If the update does not require that you restart your iMac, click the Close box to close the window and save your changes.

ADD AND REMOVE SYSTEM APPLICATIONS

Need to add or remove one or more of the system applications that shipped with your iMac? Mac OS 9 makes it easy to change the components that make up your operating system.

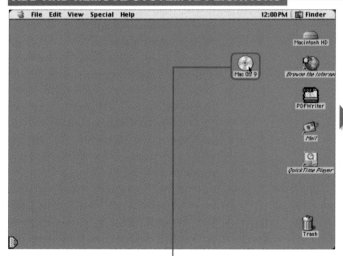

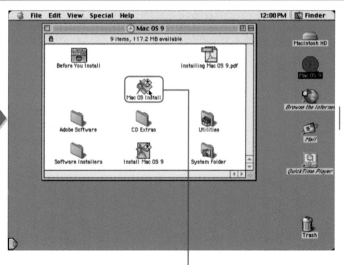

1 Insert the Mac OS 9 CD into your CD-ROM/DVD-ROM drive.

■ The CD's icon appears on the desktop.

2 Double-click the CD's icon to open it.

■ The window showing the CD's contents appears.

3 Double-click the Mac OS Install application.

What if the Install application tells me that I don't have enough space on my hard drive?

You may need to remove some other files, such as old documents or unused applications, to make room for the new items you wish to install.

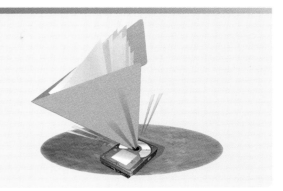

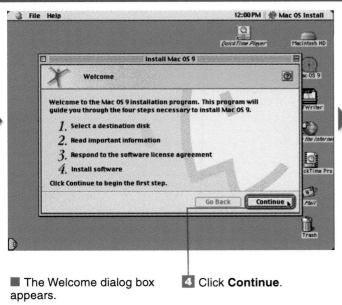

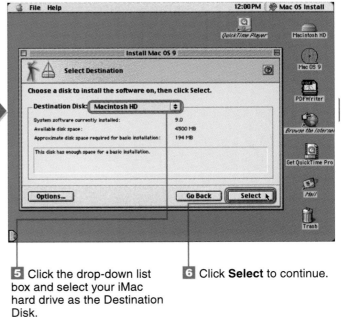

■ The Welcome dialog box appears.

4 Click **Continue**.

5 Click the drop-down list box and select your iMac hard drive as the Destination Disk.

6 Click **Select** to continue.

CONTINUED

ADD AND REMOVE SYSTEM APPLICATIONS

You can install or remove specific components of the system by using the Custom Installation and Removal dialog box.

ADD AND REMOVE SYSTEM APPLICATIONS

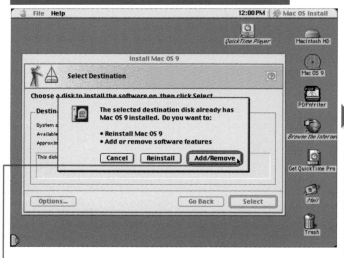

7 Click **Add/Remove**.

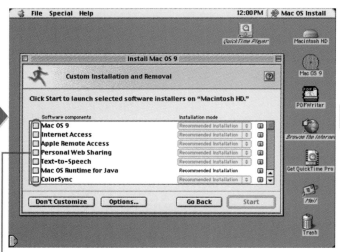

8 Click the check boxes next to the system components you want to add or remove.

How can I get more information on a software component before I install it?

Click the *i* button next to the entry to display the size and a short description of the component.

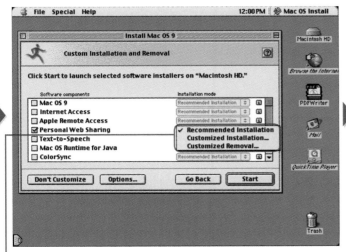

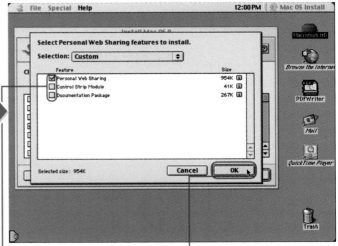

9 Click the drop-down list for the component and choose either Customized Installation or Customized Removal.

10 On the Selection screen, check the boxes next to the specific components that you want to add or remove.

11 Click **OK** to return to the Custom Installation and Removal dialog box.

12 Click **Start**.

SPECIAL STARTUP KEY COMBINATIONS

You can use a number of special key combinations when starting your iMac. These keys are often used when troubleshooting problems.

To use a startup key sequence, hold down the specified keys while you turn on your iMac, and continue to press them until you see the result of your action.

Sometimes, you may install a piece of software that adds a troublesome extension to your Extensions folder; the new extension may conflict with another extension and cause your iMac to crash or freeze.

To fix this problem, you want to restart your iMac with system extensions off. To do this, hold down the Shift key until you see the Mac OS 9 splash screen and the words *Extensions disabled*.

To start your iMac from a bootable CD-ROM or DVD, insert the disc into the drive and then choose Special⇨Restart. Then hold down the C key until you see the Mac OS 9 splash screen.

When you start up off of a different disc, such as the Mac OS 9 install disc, you may see a different background behind the splash screen and a different set of extensions load at the bottom of the screen.

Why start up without system extensions?

A buggy extension can lock up your iMac or disable system features like sound or USB devices. If you hold down the Shift key and disable extensions, you can complete the startup process and remove the program or extension causing the problem.

Every once in a while, your desktop folder may become corrupt, causing errors and weird behavior as you use your iMac. To rebuild your Mac OS desktop folder, restart your iMac and, right after the splash screen disappears and the desktop background appears, hold down the ⌘ and Option keys. Click Yes when your iMac asks if you're sure you want to rebuild the desktop.

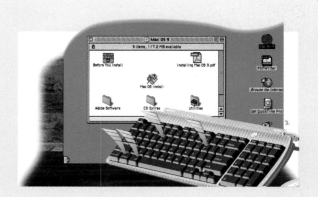

To reset many of your Control Panel settings to their defaults and clear the system parameters stored in your iMac's memory, hold down the ⌘+Option+P+R keys immediately after rebooting. After your iMac has sounded two tones, you should release the keys. Make sure you restore the Control Panel settings affected by the reset.

USING THE EXTENSIONS MANAGER

By using the Extensions Manager, you can selectively turn off individual system extensions, startup and shutdown programs, and Control Panels to track down a problem.

You can also use the Extensions Manager to disable extensions or Control Panels that you don't use, which can free up additional RAM.

USING THE EXTENSIONS MANAGER

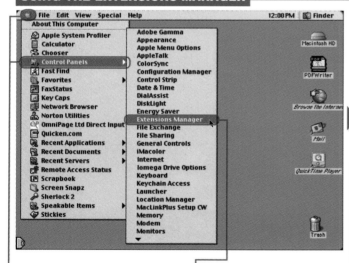

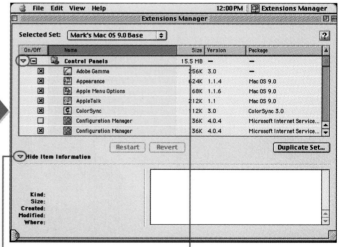

1 Click the Apple menu.

2 Choose **Control Panels**.

3 Choose **Extensions Manager**.

Note: You can find system extensions and Control Panels in their respective folders inside the System Folder.

■ The Extensions Manager dialog box appears.

4 Click the triangle next to Show Item Information.

■ This area shows valuable information about each extension.

5 Click the triangle next to the system components you'd like to change.

My iMac just froze! What can I do?

Restart your iMac while holding down the spacebar. This emergency procedure displays the Extensions Manager immediately during the startup process, so that you can troubleshoot and disable the extension that is locking up your computer.

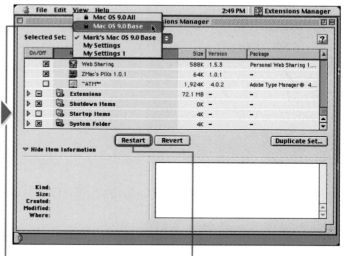

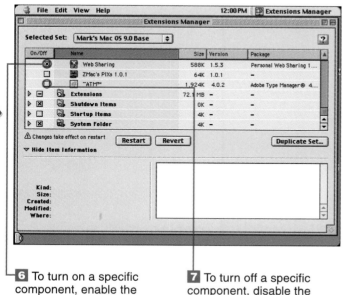

6 To turn on a specific component, enable the check box next to it.

7 To turn off a specific component, disable the check box next to it.

8 If you'd like to return to the default set of Mac OS 9 components, click the Selected Sets list and choose **Mac OS 9.0 Base**.

9 To reboot your computer with the desired changes, click **Restart**.

USING THE SYSTEM PROFILER

Before you contact Apple's technical support, try running the Apple System Profiler. This program can display a complete description of the hardware and software installed on your system, and it's a gold mine of information for a computer technician.

USING THE SYSTEM PROFILER

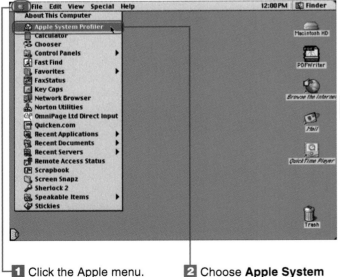

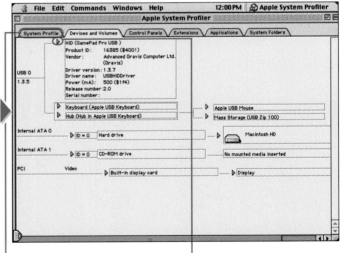

1 Click the Apple menu.

2 Choose **Apple System Profiler**.

■ The Apple System Profiler dialog box appears.

3 To display a specific hardware or software set, click the desired tab.

4 Click the triangle to show or hide details.

**I don't need all this information
right now! How can I customize
the System Profiler screen?**

Choose Edit⇨Preferences to
display the Preferences dialog
box, in which you can choose the
information the program displays.

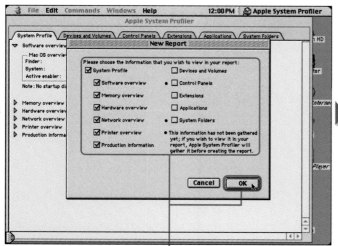

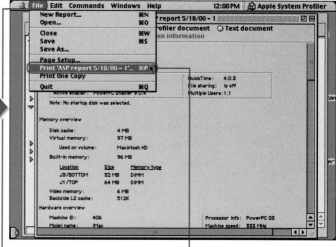

*Note: To display basic
information, such as the version
of the Mac OS you're running
and the amount of RAM available,
click the Apple menu in the Finder
and choose **About This Computer**.*

5 To generate a report,
press ⌘+N.

6 Enable the check boxes
for the information that you
want to review.

7 Click **OK**.

8 To print your system
profile, click **File**.

9 Choose **Print**.

INDEX

INDEX

INDEX

INDEX

Read Less, Learn More™

Visual

Simplified®

Simply the Easiest Way to Learn

For visual learners who are brand-new to a topic and want to be shown, not told, how to solve a problem in a friendly, approachable way.

All *Simplified*® books feature friendly Disk characters who demonstrate and explain the purpose of each task.

Title	ISBN	Price
America Online® Simplified®, 2nd Ed.	0-7645-3433-5	$24.99
Computers Simplified®, 4th Ed.	0-7645-6042-5	$24.99
Creating Web Pages with HTML Simplified®, 2nd Ed.	0-7645-6067-0	$24.99
Excel 97 Simplified®	0-7645-6022-0	$24.99
Excel for Windows® 95 Simplified®	1-56884-682-7	$19.99
FrontPage® 2000® Simplified®	0-7645-3450-5	$24.99
Internet and World Wide Web Simplified®, 3rd Ed.	0-7645-3409-2	$24.99
Lotus® 1-2-3® Release 5 for Windows® Simplified®	1-56884-670-3	$19.99
Microsoft® Access 2000 Simplified®	0-7645-6058-1	$24.99
Microsoft® Excel 2000 Simplified®	0-7645-6053-0	$24.99
Microsoft® Office 2000 Simplified®	0-7645-6052-2	$29.99
Microsoft® Word 2000 Simplified®	0-7645-6054-9	$24.99
More Windows® 95 Simplified®	1-56884-689-4	$19.99
More Windows® 98 Simplified®	0-7645-6037-9	$24.99
Office 97 Simplified®	0-7645-6009-3	$29.99
PC Upgrade and Repair Simplified®	0-7645-6049-2	$24.99
Windows® 95 Simplified®	1-56884-662-2	$19.99
Windows® 98 Simplified®	0-7645-6030-1	$24.99
Windows® 2000 Professional Simplified®	0-7645-3422-X	$24.99
Windows® Me Millennium Edition Simplified®	0-7645-3494-7	$24.99
Word 97 Simplified®	0-7645-6011-5	$24.99

Over 9 million *Visual* books in print!

with these full-color Visual™ guides

The Fast and Easy Way to Learn

Discover how to use what you learn with "Teach Yourself" tips

Title	ISBN	Price
Teach Yourself Access 97 VISUALLY™	0-7645-6026-3	$29.99
Teach Yourself Computers and the Internet VISUALLY™, 2nd Ed.	0-7645-6041-7	$29.99
Teach Yourself FrontPage® 2000 VISUALLY™	0-7645-3451-3	$29.99
Teach Yourself HTML VISUALLY™	0-7645-3423-8	$29.99
Teach Yourself the Internet and World Wide Web VISUALLY™, 2nd Ed.	0-7645-3410-6	$29.99
Teach Yourself VISUALLY™ Investing Online	0-7645-3459-9	$29.99
Teach Yourself Microsoft® Access 2000 VISUALLY™	0-7645-6059-X	$29.99
Teach Yourself Microsoft® Excel 97 VISUALLY™	0-7645-6063-8	$29.99
Teach Yourself Microsoft® Excel 2000 VISUALLY™	0-7645-6056-5	$29.99
Teach Yourself Microsoft® Office 2000 VISUALLY™	0-7645-6051-4	$29.99
Teach Yourself Microsoft® PowerPoint® 97 VISUALLY™	0-7645-6062-X	$29.99
Teach Yourself Microsoft® PowerPoint® 2000 VISUALLY™	0-7645-6060-3	$29.99
Teach Yourself More Windows® 98 VISUALLY™	0-7645-6044-1	$29.99
Teach Yourself Netscape Navigator® 4 VISUALLY™	0-7645-6028-X	$29.99
Teach Yourself Networking VISUALLY™	0-7645-6023-9	$29.99
Teach Yourself Office 97 VISUALLY™	0-7645-6018-2	$29.99
Teach Yourself Red Hat® Linux® VISUALLY™	0-7645-3430-0	$29.99
Teach Yourself Windows® 95 VISUALLY™	0-7645-6001-8	$29.99
Teach Yourself Windows® 98 VISUALLY™	0-7645-6025-5	$29.99
Teach Yourself Windows® 2000 Professional VISUALLY™	0-7645-6040-9	$29.99
Teach Yourself VISUALLY™ Dreamweaver® 3	0-7645-3470-X	$29.99
Teach Yourself VISUALLY™ iMac™	0-7645-3453-X	$29.99
Teach Yourself VISUALLY™ Windows® 2000 Server	0-7645-3428-9	$29.99
Teach Yourself Windows® Me Millennium Edition VISUALLY™	0-7645-3495-5	$29.99
Teach Yourself Windows NT® 4 VISUALLY™	0-7645-6061-1	$29.99
Teach Yourself Word 97 VISUALLY™	0-7645-6032-8	$29.99

IDG BOOKS ®

TRADE & INDIVIDUAL ORDERS

Phone: **(800) 762-2974**
or **(317) 572-3993**
(8 a.m. – 6 p.m., CST, weekdays)
FAX : **(800) 550-2747**
or **(317) 572-4002**

EDUCATIONAL ORDERS & DISCOUNTS

Phone: **(800) 434-2086**
(8:30 a.m.–5:00 p.m., CST, weekdays)
FAX : **(317) 572-4005**

CORPORATE ORDERS FOR 3-D VISUAL™ SERIES

Phone: **(800) 469-6616**
(8 a.m.–5 p.m., EST, weekdays)
FAX : **(905) 890-9434**

Qty	ISBN	Title	Price	Total

Shipping & Handling Charges

	Description	First book	Each add'l. book	Total
Domestic	Normal	$4.50	$1.50	$
	Two Day Air	$8.50	$2.50	$
	Overnight	$18.00	$3.00	$
International	Surface	$8.00	$8.00	$
	Airmail	$16.00	$16.00	$
	DHL Air	$17.00	$17.00	$

Subtotal _____

CA residents add
applicable sales tax _____

IN, MA and MD
residents add
5% sales tax _____

IL residents add
6.25% sales tax _____

RI residents add
7% sales tax _____

TX residents add
8.25% sales tax _____

Shipping _____

Total _____

Ship to:

Name_____

Address_____

Company_____

City/State/Zip_____

Daytime Phone_____

Payment: ☐ Check to IDG Books (US Funds Only)
☐ Visa ☐ Mastercard ☐ American Express

Card # _____ Exp. _____ Signature_____

maranGraphics™